The *Horse Illustrated* Guide to

TRAIL RIDING

By Micaela Myers

A Division of BowTie, Inc.
Irvine, California

Karla Austin, *Business Operations Manager*
Nick Clemente, *Special Consultant*
Barbara Kimmel, *Managing Editor*
Jarelle S. Stein, *Editor*
Jessica Knott, *Production Supervisor*
Indexed by Melody Englund

Cover photo: © CLiX Photography
The additional photos in this book are by © CLiX Photography, pp. 4, 8, 10, 18, 21, 23, 24, 27, 28, 31, 34, 37, 51, 57, 58, 62, 65, 89, 97, 100, 105, 111, 114, 125, 128, 134, 136, 139, 140, 143, 147, 148, 150, 158, 174, 177, 179, 180, 184, 187; © Moira C. Harris, 12, 41, 42, 67, 69, 71, 73, 76, 77, 82, 83, 84, 85, 156, 159, 160, 161, 163, 164, 166, 171, 172; © Dusty L. Perin, 15, 32, 36, 38, 45, 47, 48, 52, 60, 79, 86, 90, 91, 94, 96, 99, 103, 107, 110, 113, 117, 119, 130, 144, 153, 176, 182, 186, 189; © LCP, 55, 108, 127, 133

Library of Congress Cataloging-in-Publication Data

Myers, Micaela, 1974–
    The horse illustrated guide to trail riding / by Micaela Myers.
        p. cm.
    Includes bibliographical references (p.   ) and index.
    ISBN-13: 978-1-931993-95-1 (alk. paper)
    1. Trail riding. I. Title.

    SF309.28.M94 2007
    798.2'3—dc22

                                2006031984

BowTie Press®
A Division of BowTie, Inc.
3 Burroughs
Irvine, California 92618

Printed and bound in Singapore
10 9 8 7 6 5 4 3 2 1

Dedication

This book is dedicated to my mother, Anne C. Hanley, who went on countless trail rides, horse campouts, organized rides, and even a trail trial with me in my youth.

Contents

Acknowledgments 7

Introduction 9

Chapter 1: Choosing the Right Horse 11
Temperament
Training
Health
Breed
Purchasing a Trail Horse

Chapter 2: Getting the Right Stuff 35
Tack
Rider Attire

Chapter 3: In the Saddle 63
Equitation
Mounting from the Ground
Riding Up and Down Hills
Navigating Obstacles
Loosening Up with Stretches

Chapter 4: Desensitization 87
Before Beginning
Trail Gear
Trail Obstacles
Scary Objects
Water Crossings
Animals, Activities, and Vehicles
Time Well Spent

Chapter 5: Proper Planning 109
Preventive Maintenance
Preventive Grooming
Conditioning
Packing for the Trail

Contents

Health and Safety Considerations
Cooling Out

Chapter 6: In Good Company 137
Riding with Experienced Friends
Riding Etiquette with Others
Riding in a Group
Riding Alone

Chapter 7: Behavior Problems 151
Why Horses Act Up
Being Proactive
Annoying Problems
Dangerous Problems

Chapter 8: Going Places with Your Horse 175
Finding Trails in Your Area
Trailering Out for Day Rides
Camping with Your Horse
Joining a Trail Riding Group
Planned Rides

Resources 191

Glossary 195

Index 203

Acknowledgments

First and foremost, I'd like to thank my good friend and mentor Moira C. Harris for her guidance and assistance on this project. Second, sincere thanks to both my husband, Joe, for his support, and my dad, who for the past twenty-five years has helped build countless horse shelters and feed and tack rooms and even replaced my horse trailer floor. Thanks to my generous co-worker Liz Moyer for reading this manuscript and offering valuable advice. Special thanks to trainer Dale Rudin and veterinarian Nancy S. Loving for answering questions and lending their expertise. I'd also like to thank the excellent photographers whose images appear throughout this book: Moira C. Harris, Shawn Hamilton, and Dusty L. Perin. And last but not least, thanks to Lali Mitchell for housing my pony at her lovely property, complete with forest and stream, ringed by mountains of trails.

Introduction

There is nothing more relaxing than enjoying nature from the back of a contented horse. In fact, the majority of our nation's equestrians are recreational riders, not competitors. For the horse lover who is a bit of both, there are a number of trail activities to quench any competitive thirst. Although urban sprawl is eating up much of our open space, with a little research even most city dwellers can find miles of trails practically in their backyards.

This book offers all the information you need to enjoy trail riding to its fullest. Whether you're looking for a horse or already own one, we'll start with how to size up a trail candidate. From there, we'll explore the options in tack and attire so both you and your horse can be comfortable on the trail. Even though trail riding isn't a contest of who has the best form, we'll look at how you can be a better rider and make rides easier on your horse by positioning yourself and using your aids effectively. Because modern-day trail riding often means sharing the trails with others and riding on roads to access trails, this book offers detailed instruction on how to desensitize your horse. We'll also look at how to care for your trail horse and how to plan ahead to make sure you both stay healthy and happy on the trail. Riding with other horses and riders requires a bit of trail manners, so we'll discuss leading and following manners and what to do if you want to train your horse to ride out alone. Although a steady, well-trained horse is a must for the trail, even the best horses occasionally act up; we devote an entire chapter to dealing with problem behaviors on the trail. After we've discussed the training and planning aspects, we'll explore ways to find trails, to camp, and to compete in trail riding activities.

If trail riding interests you, read on for a wealth of information that will have you safely exploring trails near and far.

Choosing the Right Horse

Many characteristics define the ideal trail horse. Of course, she should have a good head on her shoulders and not be frightened of every odd noise or each unusual rock she passes. A good trail horse is also responsive to her rider, obeying subtle cues and accepting direction willingly. She should be sure-footed and sound, carrying her rider safely over rugged terrain. A trail horse also must be fit so she does not tire quickly while traversing the countryside. In addition, her gaits should be easy to sit, as her rider will be spending ample time in the saddle.

The ideal trail horse is all this, certainly, and much more. The attributes listed above fall into four general categories that must be evaluated: temperament, training, health, and breeding. Whether you already own a horse or are purchasing one for trail riding, carefully critique her suitability by looking at these four areas.

Temperament

Although training and experience can change to a certain extent how a horse handles new and unusual circumstances, horses, just like people, are born with particular temperaments. Some horses handle stress and change better than do their peers, taking it all in stride. Others get flustered or worried and prefer the security of a calmer, more predictable environment. You can train horses (and

A horse warily examines the unfamiliar brush beside the trail. A good trail horse may spook if she sees a foreign object but will quickly regain her composure.

people) to control their emotions and reactions to some degree, but you can't change their innate temperaments.

For you to enjoy trail riding, your horse also must enjoy it. You need to accept that an extremely high-strung or nervous horse probably will not be happy out on the trail, and her rider won't have a very good time either. Choose a trail horse with the following attributes:

- Calmness
- Mild reactions and quick recoveries
- Curiosity
- Independence
- Trust

Calm demeanor: A good trail horse candidate will be relaxed and laid back. You can spot these gentle, easygoing horses by their calm demeanors. A confident horse with a sensible temperament will show relaxed body language as she moves about on the lead or under saddle, whereas a nervous horse will be rigid or tense and ready to react to the slightest disturbance.

Mild reactions and quick recoveries: All horses react instinctively, usually with a flight response, to things that frighten them, but some horses respond more quickly or violently than others do. Although occasional shies are certainly forgivable, a horse that rears, bolts off uncontrollably, or spooks violently can unseat a rider and cause serious injury. A mount that puts her rider in danger is most unsuitable.

A good trail mount may spook or react to new sights and sounds but will quickly regain her composure. A horse that can recover from a scary situation willingly and move on is worth her weight in gold.

Curiosity: A good trail horse is naturally curious. She will look at unusual items or surroundings with interest rather than fear. If allowed, she will walk forward to investigate rather than bolt. Even a horse that is nervous when passing a frightening object but doesn't spin around or spook is a good candidate for trail riding.

Independence: Horses are herd animals, and as such they feel more comfortable in the company of other horses. This can be a negative. Some horses get very antsy and upset if their friends are out of sight for even a moment. You could plan on always riding with other people, but a horse confident enough to move away from her friends is an important asset—someday you might need to ride for help or to perform other tasks alone. You want a horse that will listen to you and not lose her cool the minute she's separated from other horses.

Trust: A horse that cannot put her trust in her rider or that would rather let her instincts consume her is probably not a good candidate.

Training

In addition to having the right temperament, your horse, to be safe on the trail, must listen to your aids, which means she needs to be well trained, with a solid foundation. Horses lacking basic training will be hard to control on the trail and, in some cases, dangerous.

Basic Skills

Like show horses, trail horses should be able to walk, jog, lope, back up, side-pass, stop, and turn with hand and leg cues in an arena before heading out on the trail. A trail horse also needs solid ground manners, including holding still while the rider mounts and dismounts, leading without dragging or bullying the handler, and tying safely. If a horse lacks any of these skills, some basic training is in order before you leave the safety of the stable.

Trail horses are also asked to tackle tasks and situations show horses will never encounter. A trail horse often needs to stand patiently while you open and shut a gate from the saddle. It's helpful if she knows how to ground tie as well. She'll also need to be trained to cross water; this can be daunting if the horse has never crossed water or has a genuine fear. Depending on what type of trail

A rider lopes down the trail on his mount, which is riding nicely on the bit. Solid training is a must for trail horses.

activities you plan to do with the horse, she may require additional skills. For example, if you plan to pack into or to camp in areas without corrals, you'll need a horse trained to stand hobbled or tied on a high line. Know ahead of time what you plan to use the horse for, then come up with a list of skills your candidate must possess before you take to the trails.

Training Versus Age

Age is not as important as temperament, training, and health. A four-year-old with a great deal of training and experience may be a better choice than a ten-year-old that hasn't been ridden or handled as frequently. However, older horses often have more training and experience than their youthful counterparts. Never overlook a senior horse; many horses are still trail riding well into their twenties.

Finding a Trainer

Your horse can always learn new skills. As the rider, you must also know how to correctly cue your horse. If you or your mount need to brush up on any basic skills, it's advisable to find a qualified trainer or riding instructor in your area. Quality instruction can be costly, but your life may literally depend on it, and it's one of the best horse-related investments you can make. Here are some points to consider when choosing a trainer or an instructor:

- *References.* Choose an instructor with strong references. Ask horse owners in your area who they recommend, or ask the trainer or instructor to provide references. Talk to other trail riders who have had success with this person.

- *Facilities.* Walk around the facilities. If they're dirty or unkempt or if the horses do not seem in good condition, keep looking.

- *Quality check.* Watch the trainer or instructor at work. How does he or she treat both the horses and the clients? If any methods or actions make you uneasy, trust your instincts and look elsewhere.

- *Qualifications.* Find out what qualifications the person has. Did he or she apprentice or get a certificate? As a trail rider, you may not be concerned with the trainer's or instructor's show-ring accomplishments, but you will want to choose someone with experience training trail horses and riders.

- *Methods.* What methods does the trainer or instructor use to help trail horses? For example, if your horse spooks easily, is the trainer experienced in using desensitization methods?

- *Location.* Does the trainer or instructor have access to trails on which he or she can help you and your horse with the type of riding situations you may encounter?

You'll want to consider each of these factors when choosing a trainer or an instructor. Having a trusted professional to turn to is invaluable. Not only can this person help you and your horse master the basics needed to succeed on the trail, but you can also go to him or her with questions or new challenges.

Health

Health cannot be overlooked, and no horse will enjoy her job or respond correctly and consistently if she's uncomfortable or in pain. You'll want to choose a horse that's in good general health. Few horses are entirely blemish free, and minor issues may not be a problem for your intended use, but ongoing or chronic conditions must be carefully considered and may exclude a potential candidate.

Soundness is a key concern when sizing up a trail horse. Many people retire their horses from more strenuous jobs, such as jumping and racing, to be "just trail horses." But if you plan to take long rides, go on rides over steep or difficult terrain, or compete in endurance or competitive trials, you'll need a horse that's sound and athletic. Horses with conditions such as mild navicular disease or arthritis may be fine for short trail rides over smooth terrain, but always ask your veterinarian exactly what type of exercise and how much is best, or even tolerable, for a particular horse.

Conformation, or the way a horse is built, will affect her soundness and ability to perform a particular activity well. Entire books have been devoted to horse conformation, and the more athletic you need the horse to be, the more conformation comes into play. Obviously, a trail rider can be less of a perfectionist than a halter class competitor can, but severe conformation defects can cause soundness issues down the road, especially if you plan to ride long distances or to compete. Your trainer, riding instructor, or veterinarian can help you determine if a particular horse's conformation may hinder her ability to perform the tasks you have in mind.

In the Canadian Rockies, a rider and her horse ascend a steep slope. To traverse difficult terrain or long distances, you must choose a sound mount.

Here is an overview of essential health factors to consider when choosing a trail horse:

- *Good feet.* A trail horse doesn't have the luxury of perfect arena footing. Trail riding requires travel over varying and often rough terrain, so choose a horse with good, solid, healthy feet. Your horse should have feet that are sound and will hold up well with regular maintenance.

- *Good eyesight.* A horse with failing eyesight will not be safe to ride over difficult terrain or through trees and other natural obstacles. In addition, poor eyesight will likely make a horse more nervous and easily frightened.

- *Good lung capacity.* If you plan to take long, difficult, or fast rides, your horse will benefit from having large nostrils and a good lung capacity. A horse with small nostrils, respiratory issues, or a small chest or lung capacity will become easily winded.

- *Clean legs.* Although most older horses won't have 100 per cent "clean" or blemish-free legs, a horse with a previously bowed tendon, ringbone, or other problems that may affect her soundness on the trail will need to be carefully evaluated before going on a trail.

- *A healthy back.* Many back problems are caused by a poor-fitting saddle, but a horse with a painful back for other reasons will have a hard time enjoying her work and will often act up under saddle.

Whether purchasing a horse or evaluating your current mount, address any long-term or major health issues and concerns with your veterinarian to see if they can be resolved or, if not, how they can be managed. Horses with chronic soundness problems, such as arthritis and navicular disease, may have limitations on the type of exercise they do or may require a higher level of management, including nutritional supplements, special shoeing, pain medication, and joint injections.

Breed

You'll find all breeds of horses on the trail, and any breed can potentially be a good trail horse. Although you may fancy a particular breed, the three factors mentioned before—temperament, training, and health—are most important when choosing a trail horse. Breeding will, in large part, determine what gaits your horse possesses and her general conformation, but keep in mind that this can vary a great deal from horse to horse. The temperaments of your horse's parents and grandparents often can give you an indication of what type of temperament to expect from your horse, so if you buy from a breeder, ask to meet a candidate's sire or dam, inquire about their personalities, and find out what type of activities they've been used for.

Breeding also influences a horse's size and build. If you're a large rider, you'll want to choose a horse that can easily carry your weight. Height is not the only factor to consider. Just because a horse is tall doesn't necessarily mean she will be able to carry more weight. The horse's conformation and general build, as well as her health, will also determine how much weight she can handle. In general, heavy riders need to choose larger, stouter horses. If you have an experienced friend or instructor to take horse shopping with you, this person can help you evaluate whether a potential prospect is right for you. You can also ask your veterinarian's opinion on the size match when the prepurchase exam is scheduled.

Although every breed is known for particular traits, you will find exceptions to every rule. Remember that each horse, like each person, brings her own set of attributes to the table, so evaluate every potential horse on her own merits, not by breed or color. Although one breed may be known for its great temperament, that doesn't mean all horses of that breed have great temperaments. And even breeds with a reputation for being hot or high-strung can have very mellow individuals. The following are some of the most common breeds you'll find on the trail.

A western rider lopes through an Arizona valley on his American Paint Horse gelding. This hardy, versatile, and calm breed is a favored trail horse.

American Paint Horse

Original use: Paint Horses were used to perform cattle and ranch work across the West. They have bloodlines similar to those of the American Quarter Horse.

Characteristics and trail suitability: The traditional Paint Horse features a stock horse build, with a muscular body averaging between 15 and 16 hands. The American Paint Horse is known for flashy coloring and a calm temperament.

American Quarter Horse

Original use: Quarter Horses were developed to run quarter-mile races, hence the name, but have also gone on to find great success as ranch horses and all-around mounts.

Characteristics and trail suitability: Traditionally, Quarter Horses feature a muscular, stock horse build, averaging 15 to 16 hands. As America's most popular horse, American Quarter Horses are known for being sturdy and level-headed mounts.

Appaloosa

Original use: Appaloosas were developed by the Nez Perce Indians, who prized them for their colorful spots and coat patterns. Western settlers used Appaloosas for ranch and cattle work.

Characteristics and trail suitability: This breed tends to have a muscular build, in part from the Quarter Horse blood added in modern times. Appaloosas average 14.2 to 15.2 hands in height. Among other traits, Appaloosas are known for their stamina and strong hooves.

Arabian

Original use: Best known for their stamina, Arabians are the oldest pure breed in existence. Developed on the Arabian Peninsula, the breed was used in battle and for quick travel across the deserts.

Characteristics and trail suitability: Arabians have refined, delicate features; they often have small heads, dished faces, and high tail carriage. The breed's average height is 14.2 to 15 hands. Because Arabians were bred to travel long distances swiftly, they are considered a "hot" breed, but they are also known for being friendly, intelligent, and people oriented. Arabians are the mounts of choice for many long-distance and endurance riders.

Morgan

Original use: Morgans were originally used for farm work and racing under saddle and in harness.

Characteristics and trail suitability: Standing an average of 14.2 to 15.2 hands, Morgans are known for their stamina, intelligence, and good temperaments.

Mustang

Original use: Mustangs are America's wild horses, originating from stock that escaped or was turned loose on the range.

Characteristics and trail suitability: Mustangs are considered hardy and sturdy, but be aware that horses adopted off the range will need considerable training. Most Mustangs average 13.2 to 15 hands.

Endurance world champions Becky Hart and Grand Sultan, an Arabian, cross the beach during a competition. Long-distance trail riders and competitors often choose Arabians.

An English rider and her Thoroughbred enjoy the fall foliage. The calmer-tempered members of this famous racehorse breed can make good trail mounts.

Standardbred

Original use: Standardbreds were bred as trotters or pacers to pull sulkies in harness races.

Characteristics and trail suitability: Standardbreds are known for having great temperaments. The breed features a slightly longer and leaner build than the stock horse breeds and stands on average around 15.2 hands. As with other racehorses, off-the-track Standardbreds will need considerable training before they can be suitable trail horses, but the breed is often used for trail riding, and Standardbreds are even making inroads in endurance competition.

Thoroughbred

Original use: The Thoroughbred was bred for racing and is the world's most popular racehorse. Thoroughbreds are also successful sport horses.

Characteristics and trail suitability: Thoroughbreds tend to be long and lean compared with the stock breeds, averaging 16 to 16.2 hands. Like Arabians, Thoroughbreds are considered a hot breed and can be sensitive and high strung, but Thoroughbreds with milder dispositions are often suitable for the trail. With retraining, even many ex-racehorses adapt to make good trail horses.

Gaited Breeds

Gaited breeds, meaning breeds that have a gait other than the traditional walk, trot, and canter, are increasingly popular on the trail. These breeds are known for smooth gaits that do not bounce or jostle a rider as a trot might. If you're interested in purchasing a gaited horse for trail, find an instructor who teaches on the breed you're considering, and take a few lessons. Become familiar with the breed's gaits, and arrange to take a trail ride or two.

When evaluating a gaited horse, make sure she goes into her gaits and maintains them easily and correctly. Another factor to consider is whether you plan to ride with friends who own non-gaited horses. Many gaited horses "walk" quite a bit faster than nongaited breeds, and this can present a problem on a mixed group ride.

Some of the most popular gaited breeds are discussed below.

Kentucky Mountain Saddle Horse

Original use: Kentucky Mountain Saddle Horses were developed in central and eastern Kentucky as multipurpose family, ranch, and workhorses.

Characteristics and trail suitability: The breed registry features two divisions to accommodate horses of different sizes: Class A for horses and Class B for ponies. Known for their hardiness and willingness, Kentucky Mountain Saddle Horses are bred to naturally perform a four-beat, rack-style gait that is smooth and ground covering, traveling up to 15 miles per hour.

Missouri Fox Trotter

Original use: Missouri Fox Trotters were developed for the needs of the settlers in the Ozark Mountains of Arkansas and Missouri.

Characteristics and trail suitability: Fox Trotters stand, on average, 14 to 17 hands and are known for their smooth, sliding fox trot. The gait involves the front end walking with animation, while the hind end trots with very little action. The breed is noted for being sure-footed, with strong hooves.

Paso Fino

Original use: Paso Finos were selectively bred in Puerto Rico and in Latin America to create a sturdy, smooth-gaited riding horse.

Characteristics and trail suitability: Paso Finos average 14 to 15 hands but are still noted for being able to carry large adults. Their gaits are performed at various speeds, with rapid footfall, hock action, and drive.

Peruvian Paso

Original use: The Peruvian Paso was bred to travel the rough terrain of Peru for long distances.

Characteristics and trail suitability: Peruvian Pasos perform a comfortable, lateral gait that features a round movement in the forelegs, powered by strong hind legs. Average height for the breed is between 14 and 15 hands.

Rocky Mountain Horse

Original use: The breed was developed in the mountains of eastern Kentucky as an all-purpose utility horse.

Characteristics and trail suitability: Rocky Mountain Horses are prized for their calm dispositions and smooth, four-beat natural gait that features a near-even cadence and minimal ground clearance to allow the breed to travel long distances without tiring. Rocky Mountain Horses typically stand between 14.2 and 16 hands.

Spotted Saddle Horse

Original use: Spotted Saddle Horses were selectively bred to create a riding horse with a comfortable gait and colorful coat.

Characteristics and trail suitability: All Spotted Saddle Horses must meet color requirements and exhibit a smooth saddle gait other than a trot, such as a single-foot, running walk, stepping-pace, or rack. On average, they measure 14.2 to 15.2 hands and are popular trail mounts.

With the four-beat gait of its breed, a Rocky Mountain Horse carries a rider in Kentucky. Smooth movement and generally calm temperaments make gaited breeds popular.

An Andalusian walks calmly on a lead, displaying good ground manners. If possible, catch and lead a prospective trail horse yourself to evaluate her manners.

Tennessee Walking Horse

Original use: Developed in the South, Tennessee Walking Horses were popular among plantation owners who desired a riding horse with smooth, ground-covering gaits.

Characteristics and trail suitability: Tennessee Walking Horses are medium-size horses, averaging 15 to 16 hands. Tennessee Walkers are very popular among trail riders for their calm temperaments as well as their gliding gaits. Unlike the traditional walk and trot, the Tennessee Walking Horse's smooth flat walk and running walk carry the rider swiftly forward without bouncing.

Purchasing a Trail Horse

If you already own a horse, you'll need to make an honest assessment of her suitability for trail riding. Evaluate her soundness and temperament for trail, then ensure she has solid training before expecting a quiet ride in the great outdoors. Unless you've trained horses in general and trail horses in particular, you'll want to start out with an experienced trail horse. If you don't already own a horse, take your time and choose your new trail horse carefully.

Evaluating a Horse

You'll probably begin your search for a horse by looking through ads from the paper, Internet, or local tack-store bulletin boards. Below are tips on searching for and evaluating horses.

Search Tips

Here are a few tips to help you with your search:

Evaluate the horse's description: Look for horses advertised as good on trail. Most ads will say what the horse has previously been used for, so stick to the ones that indicate the horse already has competence outside the arena.

Call for more information: Find out exactly what trail experience the horse has had to see if it matches what you plan to do with her. For example, if you're looking for a good pleasure horse that enjoys a few miles on the trail, horses currently competing in 100-mile endurance races are not the best match. Find a horse that will be happy doing what you would like to do.

Schedule a visit: If the horse sounds like a good match, schedule a test ride and take an experienced friend, a trainer, or a riding instructor with you. This person can help you determine if the horse is appropriate for you in temperament and training. You may want to ask your companion to videotape the ride. That way, you can review the tape later to discuss the horse as a potential candidate in greater detail or to compare the horse with other prospects.

Evaluation Tips

Take your time during your evaluation. Don't let the seller pressure you. If you are not allowed to thoroughly test out the prospect, move on. Here are some tips for evaluating your trail horse candidate:

Get the horse yourself: Ask to go get the horse from her pen yourself, groom her, saddle her and bridle her, or watch the owner perform these tasks to evaluate how the horse handles them. Her ground manners are just as important as her behavior under saddle.

Note her ground manners: If she doesn't tie or has a bad attitude, note these facts. It's inconvenient to have a horse that won't tie or have to retrain one to tie, and tying will be necessary in many situations. It's always safer to have a horse that will tie well on trail rides in case of an emergency or even if you want to stop for lunch. A bad attitude about being handled and ridden could indicate physical pain or reflect the horse's overall temperament.

Let the owner ride first: Watch the owner ride the horse in an arena (or paddock if an arena is not available) to show you what the horse can do. A horse that doesn't willingly walk, jog, lope, sidepass, turn, stop, and back up should not be considered.

Ride in the ring: Once the owner has demonstrated that the horse knows her basics, ride her yourself, asking her again to walk,

These two horses work well together, neither one acting up. Evaluate how well a prospective trail mount interacts with other horses before purchasing.

As the slack in the lead and relaxed position of the head indicate, this horse has no problem calmly exiting the trailer on command.

jog, lope, side-pass, turn, stop, and back up. A horse that performs for her owner but does not respond to you may not be a good match for your riding level.

Trail ride: If all goes well and you still think the horse is a good candidate, see if you can take the horse on the trail. If the owner does not have another horse that he or she can ride on the trail with you, or if you plan to ride the horse alone on the trail, ask the owner to walk along with you while you go out for a ride. Even a short trail ride in the field next door will help you get a feel for how the horse handles when leaving the confines of an arena.

Assess her trail skills: The more you can test the horse, the better. If you can, see how the horse deals with traffic and water crossings.

Test her trailer loading: If possible, ask if you can watch the horse being loaded into a trailer. Even if you don't plan to trailer her often, you'll need to do so in an emergency and, of course, when you take her home (if you decide to buy her). You want a horse that will calmly enter and exit the trailer.

Prepurchase Exam

Once you've thoroughly evaluated your candidate and are happy with the results, it's time to call the veterinarian. As with any horse purchase, a trail horse should receive a prepurchase examination from your veterinarian (or a veterinarian recommended by a trusted friend—not the current owner's veterinarian to avoid a conflict of interest). Although the prepurchase examination will cost you extra cash, it could save you hundreds in the long run if the horse has a problem that is not obvious. During the prepurchase exam, the horse's general health and soundness are evaluated. The veterinarian can also confirm the horse's approximate age.

Most horses are not 100 percent perfect or "clean," and the veterinarian may find problems in the exam. This doesn't necessarily mean you should rule out the horse, but make sure you understand any limitations the horse may have and the prognosis for her health and usability. Tell the veterinarian exactly what you plan to do with the horse so that he or she can determine if the horse is physically up to the task.

This careful selection will help ensure that you and your trail horse have a long and satisfying partnership. Once you have found your future trail horse, it is time to take her home and get to work preparing for all the enjoyment and adventure trail riding offers.

Getting the Right Stuff

What your horse and you wear on the trail is about far more than looks. Picking the correct tack and the correct attire will ensure your horse's comfort and safety and your own. The choices in colors, materials, and styles can seem daunting, but the only two factors that really matter are fit and function.

Your tack—saddle, bridle, and bit—allows you to communicate with your horse, so choosing the right equipment and making sure it fits properly are imperative. Your attire—boots, pants, helmet, gloves, jacket, and such—allow you to comfortably and safely spend a day on the trail. Keep in mind that on the trail, you're not restricted by the rules of the show arena, so you'll find trail riders using English equipment and attire, western equipment and attire, or a combination. What matters is that your choice works well for you and your horse.

Tack

Finding the right equipment will probably be a process of trial and error. If the horse came with a bridle or a saddle, this can be a good place to start. Keep in mind, however, that the horse may have been at a different training stage; the tack may not fit the horse correctly; or you may find the previous owner's choices unsuitable for the way you ride.

If you have a trusted horse trainer or riding instructor, ask this person for recommendations, such as what bit might be best, based on your horse's training and your riding experience. Perhaps you or your friends already own a variety of saddles, bits, and bridles and can simply try a number of pieces to find out what works and what fits best.

Saddles

The saddle will most likely be your most expensive piece of tack. Purchase it with care: your comfort and that of your horse depend greatly on it. Trail saddles include western types designed specifically for trail, endurance saddles, and Australian stock saddles. Which you choose will depend on your personal preference, the type of trail riding you plan to do, and the makes and models that best fit your horse.

Whatever type of saddle you choose, proper fit is essential. The importance of a correctly fitting saddle cannot be overemphasized. An ill-fitting saddle can cause your horse all kinds of pain and result in any number of bad behaviors.

Shown here from left to right are an Australian stock saddle, an endurance saddle, and a western saddle, all of which are commonly used on trail.

This western saddle fits well and is properly placed: it does not tip forward or backward, and the seat is the lowest point.

Types of Saddles

Trail saddles are often lighter in weight than traditional western saddles and may feature built-in perks, such as a gel or cushioned seat and added D-ring attachments for fastening saddlebags and other accessories. Some trail saddles also offer rounded or cutaway skirts for heat reduction, and many do not have horns that could get in the way when you lean forward going up a steep hill.

Endurance saddles are the saddle of choice for long-distance riders. Endurance saddles look similar to western saddles, minus the horn, and feature rounded or cutaway skirts to help the horse stay cool on long rides. To allow the rider to post easily when trotting, the seat on an endurance saddle may not be as deep as the one on a

A saddle rack displays a saddle made from synthetic materials rather than leather. This type of saddle is often lighter and easier to maintain.

western saddle. Australian stock saddles have attributes of both English and western saddles and can also be comfortable for trail riding.

Western saddles are usually heavier than trail saddles and may place the rider farther back on the horse, which can be more tiring for the horse on long-distance rides. However, for general trail and pleasure riding, western saddles are a popular choice. The horn and saddle strings on this type of saddle provide places to attach saddlebags and other equipment. Western saddles come in a variety of styles specialized for different events, including equitation, barrel racing, pleasure, and cutting; there's nothing wrong with using one of these on trail if you find it comfortable and it fits your horse well. Each of these styles is designed for a different use and discipline, which will affect your position in the saddle.

Although English saddles are not as common among trail riders, some riders choose to use them. They offer riders more freedom of movement but less security than other saddle types do. English saddles also have fewer attachment options for riders wanting to add saddlebags or carry a jacket.

You may even find bareback riders on trail. However, given that the trail environment is unpredictable, it's best to have the added security of a saddle. Bareback riding on trail should be left to only the most experienced riders.

Most saddles are available in leather and synthetic versions. The choice is up to you. You should consider weight with any type of saddle you buy, and some synthetic saddles are lighter than their leather counterparts. In addition, although leather saddles are long lasting, you will need to maintain, clean, and condition your leather. Synthetic saddles often can be hosed down and are not usually damaged by water.

Cinches, or girths, and saddle pads are available in a number of materials. Choose sizes and styles that work best for you, your horse, and your saddle. Saddle pads must have adequate cushioning, but don't make the mistake of thinking extra padding will compensate for a poor-fitting saddle. Whatever pad and cinch you choose, make sure to keep it clean—dirt and debris will irritate your horse's skin.

Fit

The saddle must, of course, fit you as well as your horse, and rider fit is usually easy to determine. Adult seat sizes are measured in inches: 15, 15½, 16, 17, and so on. English and western saddles are measured differently: if you're comfortable in a 15-inch western seat, you'll probably need a 17-inch English seat. You can sit in different seat sizes at a tack store. Choose a size that allows you adequate room. A good rule of thumb for a western saddle is that you should be able to lay your hand flat between your upper thigh and the pommel, or front rise of the saddle. For English saddles, you should be able to lay your hand flat in the saddle area in front of you and behind you. Beyond this basic seat size, the particular saddle you choose must feel comfortable. Some saddles will place your legs farther forward or back, so always ride in a saddle before deciding whether it's right for you.

For your horse, you'll find that saddles come in several tree widths to fit varying back sizes. A saddletree is the basic frame of the saddle. On a western saddle, the underside is covered with sheepskin, while an English saddle is covered with leather. You'll feel the bars (the two long pieces of wood or synthetic material that rest along your horse's back on either side of his spine) but not see them. Saddletree widths and the resulting bar angles commonly are available in Quarter Horse or semi–Quarter Horse sizes on western saddles (you may also see Arabian and draft trees). English saddles usually come in narrow, medium or standard, and wide. Unfortunately, the angles are not standardized, so a medium in one saddle brand may fit like a narrow in another. There are also new treeless saddle options. Some horses and riders find these comfort-

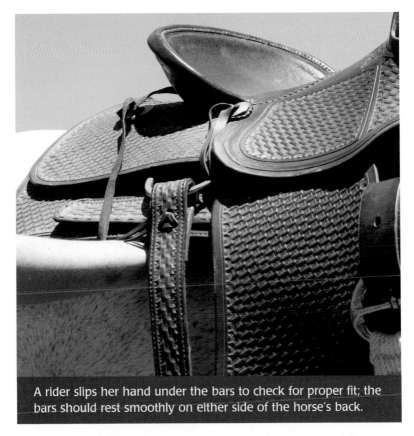

A rider slips her hand under the bars to check for proper fit; the bars should rest smoothly on either side of the horse's back.

able, whereas others do not. Carefully evaluate any saddle you're considering purchasing.

If you're buying a new saddle, bring in pictures of your horse and describe his back and withers so the tack store employees can help you determine which size to try first. You can buy products to draw and record the shape of your horse's back to take to a tack store with you. Whether you buy new or used, you'll need to try the saddle on your horse before you know whether it fits. Most tack stores will let you do this provided you return the saddle in the same condition. Don't buy from a store that doesn't allow you to take the saddle home and return it if it doesn't fit your horse.

Trained tack store employees, riding instructors, horse trainers, and veterinarians can help you determine whether your saddle fits correctly, and hiring a professional saddle fitter to come to your stable to evaluate your fit will give you complete peace of mind. However, here are a few obvious points to check:

- From the side, make sure the saddle is not tipping forward or back like a teeter-totter. The seat should be level, and it should be the deepest (lowest) point of the saddle on the horse's back.

- The gullet (front, arch-shaped part of the saddle) should allow adequate clearance so it does not rest on or touch the horse's withers.

The pad beneath this saddle has been pulled up into the gullet before the cinch is tightened so the gullet doesn't put pressure on the withers.

- Set your saddle on your horse without a pad or cinch (you can lay a clean towel down if you don't want to dirty the saddle). With your hand flat, feel under the bars of the saddle. The bars should be resting smoothly on either side of the horse's back. Bars that are too wide or too narrow will pinch and will not distribute weight evenly.

- The saddle skirts should not interfere with the horse's hip (which can happen if your saddle or its skirts are too big).

- Watch your horse's behavior. If he flinches when you set the saddle down or becomes cranky when you tighten it up or mount, he may be telling you his back hurts or his saddle doesn't fit. However, some horses are just "cinchy" from the cinch or girth being tightened too quickly or from past negative experiences. Misbehavior under saddle also may be an indication of poor saddle fit or back pain.

Make sure you place your saddle correctly as well. Start with it too far forward, then slide it back to where it naturally stops. Pull the pad up into the gullet so it doesn't restrict the withers when the cinch is tightened. Then feel for the top, back part of your horse's shoulder bone to make sure his shoulder can move freely forward and back without the saddle bars interfering. Even though the front leather part of the saddle may cover this part of the shoulder bone, make sure that the bars themselves are not resting on this bone.

Always tighten your horse's cinch, or girth, slowly. At first make it just snug enough to keep the saddle from tipping. Wait a few moments or walk your horse before tightening it another couple of notches or inches. Finally, before you mount, check it again to see if it needs to be tightened again. Never pull it so tight that you're using all of your strength. After you've ridden a while, you may need to retighten it a tad. You can check if your cinch is too loose by standing in the stirrups and bouncing your weight gently into one stirrup more than the other. If the saddle begins to move that way, you need to check your cinch. However, a saddle will naturally have more side-to-side movement on a horse with a round back and without prominent withers.

Bridles

A bridle consists of a bit, headstall, and reins. The successful combinations of the three you can put together are endless. However, as you choose a bridle, prioritize carefully. Your first priority should be how the bridle fits: Does the bit fit your horse, and is the headstall adjustable enough to fit correctly? Second, consider function: Will the bridle serve the purpose you need it for? For example, if you want to easily tie your horse, does the bridle have a built-in halter? Last, choose a bridle that is appealing to you, with reins that comfortably fit in your hands and that requires a level of care you're willing to offer.

Types of Bits

There are hundreds, if not thousands, of bit variations, and the choices can be overwhelming. However, there are several major groups or types of bits to help you narrow down your search. Finding the right bit for you and your horse may be a process of trial and error. Your horse will most likely need different bits for the various stages of his life and training as well.

For the most part, bits with thinner mouthpieces or twists (ridges) in the mouthpiece are more severe than bits with smooth, large, round, light, or hollow mouthpieces; however, the shape and size of a horse's mouth may dictate he will be more comfortable in a thinner mouthpiece. Some bits include copper, which encourages salivation to keep the horse's mouth moist and lubricated. Rounded mouthpieces, which curve up toward the top of the horse's mouth, offer extra room for the tongue.

Snaffles: In general, snaffle bits feature a joint in the middle and a D-shaped or circular ring on either end. Snaffles are direct pressure bits, meaning pressure goes directly from your hands to the bars of

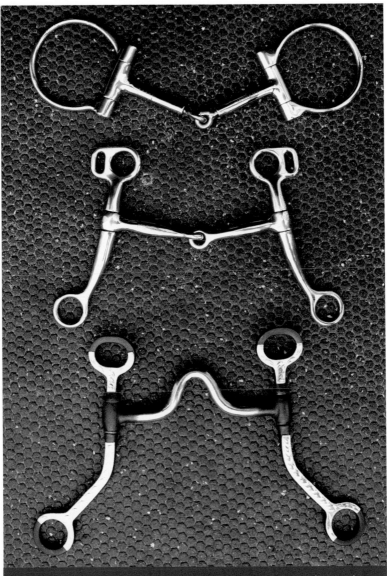

A snaffle (top) is a direct pressure bit; a Tom Thumb (middle) has shanks, making it a leverage bit; a curb bit (bottom), also a leverage bit, has a port mouthpiece and shanks.

the horse's mouth, tongue, and lips. Snaffles are popular for English riders and for young horses. Beginning riders also may choose a gentle snaffle, as these can be more forgiving of fumbling hands than leverage bits. When riding in a snaffle, you can keep light contact with the bit (meaning you can "feel" the horse's mouth).

Curb bits: Curb bits feature shanks that drop down from the mouthpiece several inches, making the curb a leverage bit. Your reins attach to the end of the shanks, and when you pull back, the shanks come back, putting pressure on your horse's chin, his poll (behind his ears), the bars of his mouth, and the roof of his mouth (via the port). Curb bits are used with a chin or curb strap (or chain) that runs from the upper rings on either side of the bit behind the horse's chin. You should be able to fit two fingers held sideways in between the chin strap and your horse's chin when no pressure is being exerted on the reins.

What height and width of port you choose will depend on the size and shape of the inside of your horse's mouth, his training, and your experience as a rider. Generally, high, thin ports should be used only on very well-trained horses for a specific purpose and will take a delicate touch from the rider. The length and angle of the shanks, as well as the purchase (the part of the shank above the bit), also will influence how pressure is applied to the horse's mouth. Some curb bits include a roller in the port, which can encourage salivation, and some horses with a "busy mouth" enjoy rolling. Young or untrained horses should never be ridden in any curb bit, and inexperienced riders with unsteady hands should avoid them as well.

Because curb bits are leverage bits, applying pressure to several parts of the horse's mouth and head, you should not ride with constant pressure on the reins. Instead, you'll keep a slight loop or drape in the reins, holding them at a length where you can close your fingers or move your hand back an inch or two and have light contact.

Tom Thumbs: Tom Thumb bits look like snaffles with shanks, but don't let this fool you into thinking they're gentle. The combination of shanks, a jointed mouthpiece, and a chin strap give the Tom Thumb a viselike action that can be very severe. Only experienced riders with gentle hands should consider a Tom Thumb.

Hackamores: Some trail riders choose mechanical hackamores—not to be confused with a traditional hackamore, which features a rawhide noseband sometimes used in the early stages of a western horse's training. Mechanical hackamores are made with a flat or braided piece of leather that goes over the horse's nose and attaches to a curb or chin strap (or chain) and long metal shanks. Although you may think they're a gentler choice than a bit, mechanical hackamores exert pressure on the horse's nose, poll, and chin and should not be used by beginning riders or those with unsteady hands. As with leverage bits, you should not ride with constant pressure on the reins when using a hackamore.

Bit Fit

The bit is the most important part of your bridle, as it will play a major part in communicating with your horse. Before purchasing

A rider compares a string measurement of the horse's mouth with the bit to make sure the bit isn't too narrow or too wide.

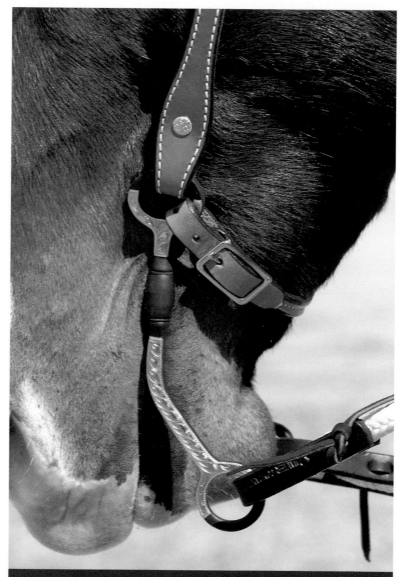

Your bit should be adjusted so that you have only one or two wrinkles or smile lines at the corner of your horse's mouth, as shown here.

any bit, you'll first need to determine what size your horse needs. Bits are measured in inches across, such as 4½ or 5 inches, based on the width of your horse's mouth. To measure, run a piece of string through your horse's mouth where the mouthpiece will go, from one outside corner of his lip to the other. Insert the string from the front of his mouth, just as you would a bit, keeping the string taut. Add three-quarters of an inch to the measurement you get. The number you come up with should allow you to buy a bit that is wide enough to not pinch the sides of your horse's mouth but not so wide it rattles or wiggles from side to side.

In addition to width, how you adjust the bit in the horse's mouth will influence its effectiveness and your horse's comfort. Generally, you want one wrinkle or smile line at the corner of your horse's mouth, where his lips meet the mouthpiece. You don't want the bit dangling in his mouth (too low) or pinching his lips (too high).

Aside from these bit-fit basics, other factors to consider are your horse's teeth and his inner mouth. If your horse has problems wearing bits, you'll want your veterinarian to rule out any health issues with his teeth or mouth (including previous damage to his bars, the area where the bit rests). Next, have your veterinarian or an experienced trainer help you evaluate the inside of your horse's mouth to determine what shape of bit and mouthpiece may fit him best. Such factors as how large your horse's tongue is, how shallow or deep his palate (top of his mouth) is, and the amount of space between his top and bottom bars all play into how comfortable a particular bit will be for him. Of course, horses also must be trained to accept a bit and give to pressure as part of their basic training.

Headstalls

After you've chosen your bit, you must decide on the best headstall to hold it in place. Western headstalls come in split ear and browband versions. Split ear headstalls feature a loop around one or both of the horse's ears instead of a browband, which goes across the horse's forehead. Split ear styles generally do not have throatlatches, as browband styles do. A throatlatch goes under your horse's throat and should be adjusted so you can fit four fingers sideways between the flat, round part of your horse's cheekbone and the strap. You want your horse to be able to tuck his chin without the throatlatch's being too tight, but you don't want it so loose it won't do its job, which is to help secure the headstall.

If you're using a snaffle, you may want to choose an English headstall, which in addition to a browband and throatlatch features a cavesson—a strap that buckles around your horse's nose, two to three finger widths below the thin, protruding face bone. You can also ride with a snaffle on a western headstall, but make sure the headstall features a browband, a throatlatch, and a chin strap. The chin strap on a snaffle should be adjusted loosely, as its only job is to help steady the snaffle and keep it from being pulled through the horse's mouth in an extreme case. The chin strap has a more important role when used with a curb bit. When adjusting the chin strap on a curb bit, you should be able to place only two fingers held sideways between your horse's chin and the strap. This will ensure the strap can do its job without being too tight.

Make sure any headstall is adjustable to fit your horse's head without pinching, rubbing, or hanging too loosely. Headstalls come in several sizes, including pony, cob, Arabian, horse, and oversize. A hole punch is always good to have on hand should you need to make additional adjustments.

Halter-bridle combinations are great for trail riders. This type of headstall has a halter built into the bridle. A combo halter-bridle allows you to tie the horse using a halter without carrying one along or changing from bridle to halter. You can also unclip the bit to allow your horse to graze when you stop for a break.

You never want to tie a horse by the reins. If he gets frightened and pulls back with a bit in his mouth, it can cause severe damage to the bars of his mouth.

A Hanoverian mare wears an English headstall and a snaffle bit, which work best together because the cavesson around the nose steadies the whole bridle.

Most headstalls come in nylon and in leather. Nylon has the advantage of being easy to clean, as you can usually hand wash it or run it through your washing machine's gentle cycle. Water won't damage nylon the way it does leather. However, many people prefer the look and feel of leather over nylon, and well-cared-for leather can last many years.

Reins

Western reins come in three basic varieties: split, romal, and connected. Split and romal reins are the types used in western rail show classes; the connected or single loop varieties are the type you may see in events such as barrel racing.

Split reins feature two separate reins, one on each side of the bit. If you are riding one handed, say with your left hand, the right rein

These connected western reins, a sound choice for trail riders, buckle around this horse's neck in a single loop.

would go between your thumb and pointer finger, while the left rein goes between your pointer and middle finger; then the two reins run together through the palm of your hand where they dangle on the left side of the horse. Your knuckles should face forward when riding one handed.

If you're riding two handed with split reins, you would cross the right rein over the left side of your horse's neck and the left rein over the right side, then pick up the doubled reins, one in each hand. That way, if you drop the reins with one of your hands, you won't have a single rein hanging down to the ground. Many trail riders choose to tie the ends of their split reins in a knot to prevent one rein from dropping accidentally.

Romal reins join together at the top, generally at a metal ring, and a long tail, or romal, attaches to the ring. Romal reins are meant to be used one handed. If you are holding the reins with your left hand, you would grasp them below the ring where the romal attaches, holding them in a loose fist, with the romal side coming out of the top of your hand, as if you're holding an ice cream cone in your fist. The tail, or romal, end is held in the spare hand, in this case your right hand, on your thigh. Romal reins are not commonly used on trail, but connected or single loop reins are.

Connected western reins are generally one long rein that buckles from one side of the bit to the other. These are handy, as there's no danger of one rein dropping. One end of the connected rein may have a snap so it can be used as a lead rope. Western connected reins are often adjustable, allowing you to make them longer or shorter depending on your needs. English reins, which buckle in the middle at the horse's withers, can also be used on trail but do not allow for length adjustment.

As with bridles, you can find reins in nylon and in leather; there are also rubber grip versions. Reins can be thick or thin and vary in length. Choose the size, style, and material that work best for you and your horse.

Training Aids

For general trail riding, training devices—such as tie-downs, draw reins, and martingales—are best left at home. Tie-downs and draw reins have their places in the training pen but not out on trail. Tie-downs are used mainly by speed horses, such as barrel racers, to brace against for fast turns. They are not meant to force a horse's head into position or to keep him from rearing. If your horse has behavioral issues, go back to basics with arena training rather than reaching for a "gadget." Draw reins are often used to help a horse learn to carry himself in a proper frame but should be used only by experienced hands in the arena. Running martingales, which feature straps that come up from a horse's chest and rings that the reins run through, are popular among endurance competitors. However, they are not standard equipment for the average trail rider and require knowledgeable adjustment and use.

Spurs can be helpful to cue a horse or encourage him to respect your leg, but only if you already have a steady leg. Beginning riders should never use spurs, as they may accidentally jab the horse with the spurs when their legs bounce or move. Experienced riders can use a spur to gently remind a horse if he doesn't listen to the initial squeeze from the calf. Always accustom your horse to spurs in the arena before using them on trail. Avoid long, sharp spurs on trail, as they could accidentally jam into your horse's side should he run your leg into a tree or other object.

Additional Tack

Additional tack includes saddlebags, seat cushions, safety stirrups, breast collars and cruppers, and leg protection, as well as other equipment.

Saddlebags: Saddlebags come in all shapes and sizes. Some fit behind your seat, others on the front or the horn. Even if you take only short rides, you'll need at least a small saddle or horn bag for the essentials and possibly a water bottle holder. Insulated bags are available if you choose to pack hot or cold food and beverages.

A red saddlebag fits snugly behind a seat. The saddle also has a sheepskin cushion that provides needed comfort on long trail rides.

Seat cushions: If the saddle you purchase doesn't have a built-in gel or cushioned seat and you plan to take long rides, it's advisable to purchase an add-on seat cushion. There are gel seat cushions as well as sheepskin versions. Some sheepskin seat covers go all the way down over the western saddle's fenders (pieces of leather you rest your legs against), while other cover just the seat itself. Additional padding can help prevent your seat bones from becoming sore and achy on long rides.

Safety stirrups: Safety or specialty stirrups are another add-on to consider. Safety stirrups are designed to release your foot if you fall. With regular stirrups, you can be dragged behind the horse if your foot becomes lodged or stuck during a fall. Safety stirrups are available in a variety of types and styles in both western and English versions; however, western safety stirrups are not as common. You can also purchase wider stirrups, padded stirrups, or padded inserts, which may alleviate knee pain.

Breast collars and cruppers: Many trail riders use a breast collar (available in nylon and in leather) to help prevent their saddles from slipping back when riding uphill. A breast collar attaches to small metal D-rings on either side of the saddle and runs across his chest. Some versions also have a strap that goes between the horse's legs and attaches to the cinch. Choose a breast collar that's relatively wide for added support and comfort. A breast collar shouldn't be tight like a cinch or hang down loosely where it will get caught under the point of the horse's shoulders. A well-fitted breast collar should run just above the horse's shoulder blades, where it won't interfere with his movement. Make sure it's not too high, either, as this could affect your horse's breathing. The breast collar should lay flat against your horse's coat all around, without sagging or digging in. Avoid breast collars that run straight across the horse's chest, as this can restrict his shoulder movement.

If you have a horse with a very round back and withers, you may need a crupper. Cruppers feature a leather or synthetic strap

A wide breast collar stretches across a palomino's upper chest. Adjust breast collar straps carefully so that they do not cause rubbing.

These red splint boots, worn on the forelegs, help prevent interference injuries. Bell boots, shown around the top of the hoof, prevent forging, or striking one foot against another.

that runs from the back of your saddle and underneath the base of your horse's tail to prevent the saddle from slipping forward.

Leg protection: Depending on your horse's needs, you may choose to place protective leg wear, such as splint boots, sport boots, or bell boots on him. If your horse tends to overreach or forge and hit his front heels with his hind feet, bell boots are necessary. Splint boots will be needed if your horse interferes or strikes one front leg with the opposite front hoof. Sport boots can support a horse's legs, and performance riders often use them, as do many trail riders. Some models have boot covers to keep plants and debris from sticking to them. Avoid riding your horse in wet or dirty boots, as they can cause irritation. Watch out for very sandy soil as well; sand can get in between the boots and your horse's leg, causing abrasion.

Safety additions: If you ride during deer hunting season, you may choose to outfit your horse in bright orange gear, such as a tassel, a halter, a breast collar, or a saddle pad. Although hunters rarely shoot horses accidentally, it has happened. A number of manufacturers sell bright orange tack. Reflective gear is also available if you ride at night, dawn, or dusk.

Rider Attire

When it comes to attire, trail riders have a lot more freedom than arena competitors do. To be comfortable and safe trail riding, however, you will need to put some thought into your wardrobe. Boots with a heel are a must—they keep your foot from sliding too far and possibly becoming lodged in the stirrup. Boots designed for riding, whether they're western, English, tall, short, lace-up, zip-up, or pull-on, are your best choices. They'll be the correct size for fitting in stirrups, will have an adequate heel, and will have the right sole. Most riding boots are smooth on the bottom to facilitate easy entry to and exit from the stirrup. However, multipurpose boots, such as those used for stable chores and riding, may have some traction. If you ride in the winter, consider purchasing a second pair of insulated boots.

Although you'll see some brave trail riders in shorts on a sunny day, rubbing and chafing are likely when skin meets leather. Jeans are always a great option, especially those with a smooth inner seam for riders. Breeches or riding tights are also good choices. Avoid shirts that are so big, long, or bulky they could get caught on objects such as passing branches. A well-fitted shirt is your best bet. Specialty fabrics designed to wick, or remove, sweat can help you stay cool and dry in hot weather.

This rider's attire—long pants, tucked-in shirt, riding boots, and ASTM/SEI approved riding helmet—will provide maximum comfort and safety.

During the rainy season, you'll want to carry a waterproof jacket or slicker. Those designed for riders often feature a vented back to fit over the saddle's cantle. You can also purchase lightweight, foldable windbreakers, which can be easily stored in your saddlebag or tied behind your saddle. Gloves are optional, but many trail riders choose soft, well-fitted gloves to protect their hands.

Finally, you'll need an approved safety helmet. While trail riding may seem like a "safe" activity, a large percentage of riding accidents occur during leisure or pleasure riding—not while participating in "dangerous" sports such as jumping. Even the best rider on the quietest horse can fall off, and you have little control of external circumstances on the trail. You never know what you'll encounter, and every horse spooks at something. Wearing a helmet vastly reduces your chances of a serious head injury. Modern helmets are lightweight, affordable, and come in styles especially for trail riders, with features such as a longer visor for sun protection. Whatever model you choose, make sure it's ASTM/SEI approved. (The American Society for Testing and Materials sets safety standards for private industry helmets; the Safety Equipment Institute tests such helmets to ensure that they meet the ASTM standards.) Avoid used helmets that may have been damaged in a fall and unapproved helmets, which are more for looks than protection.

All the choices in tack and attire offer today's trail rider more options and innovation than ever before. With some careful thought and research, you can find just the right items to keep you and your horse comfortable and safe on trail.

In the Saddle

Riders are not passengers; they are partners. If you've ever seen a horse shake a tiny patch of skin to rid herself of an irritating fly, you realize how sensitive horses are. Every move the rider makes with her seat or legs is felt by the horse, and the bit and reins accentuate hand and upper body movements. Whatever your riding level, it's important to consider your impact and influence on your horse and strive to improve your communication—something you'll both be thankful for.

Equitation

Your horse should be responsive and well schooled in the arena or around your property before you venture out on trail. She should walk, jog, lope, stop, turn, back up, and side-pass on command, and she must stand still without fidgeting when asked. If she lacks these basics, consider working with an experienced riding instructor or trainer in your area.

Your horse isn't the only one that will need to be well schooled. To ride safely on trail, you'll need a steady position, good balance, and practiced aids—legs, seat, hands, and voice. Your legs and seat influence your horse's speed and direction, while your hands can help guide her head and front end and back up cues given by the legs and seat. Voice is an often-forgotten aid that can lessen your reliance on your legs, seat, and hands. Although your equitation, or proper riding, won't be judged on trail, it's imperative for your comfort and safety as well as your horse's. A well-balanced rider is easier for the horse to carry and can ride longer with fewer aches and pains. In addition, this rider is less likely to tumble off should the horse bolt, buck, or spook.

Legs

Assess your position in the saddle by first checking your alignment. There should be a straight line running from your ear, through your shoulder and hip, to your heel. Think of your body parts as building blocks, each block supporting the next. When your legs are underneath you, they'll help support your weight, absorb concussion, and keep you centered over the horse's movement.

Your heels should be lower than your toes, but never force them into a locked position. Keeping your heels down will help anchor you in the saddle, and keeping your ankles loose and relaxed will help absorb shock. Adjust your western stirrups so there's only a slight bend in your knee. English riders generally adjust their stirrups so the irons hit their anklebones when their legs are hanging and relaxed.

Your toes should point forward, allowing your inner calves, knees, and thighs to rest against the horse. This will help guide her and keep the lines of communication open. If your toes are turned out, your knees will also point out, and you'll lose contact with the horse. Remember that you want to keep her channeled between your legs.

Horses are trained to move away from pressure, so you can use your legs to move your horse over, speed her up, or bend her. Always start with the mildest cue possible, such as a gentle squeeze from your calf. Use both calves to channel your horse straight and encourage her to speed up. Always keep your heels down when using your legs. It's more effective to turn your toe out and heel in than to bring your heel up.

If you want your horse to move a shoulder, use one leg at the girth to push the front of her body in the direction desired—left leg to move right, right leg to move left. To move her hind end, use your

Astride a Quarter Horse in Kentucky, this equestrian demonstrates the proper riding position: a straight line from the ear to the shoulder and to the hip to the heel.

leg just behind the girth. If your horse doesn't listen to a gentle squeeze, increase the pressure to a firm squeeze, then a tap, and eventually a firm kick. You want to teach your horse that if she listens to a squeeze, she won't get a kick.

Always release the pressure from your legs the minute you get a response from your horse. Some riders develop "nagging" legs that constantly squeeze or bump the horse. This will dull your horse's sides and teach her to ignore your legs because they don't mean anything. Your horse's reward is for you to stop squeezing, bumping, or kicking, so do so the moment your horse responds to your cue.

Check your leg position frequently. You shouldn't be able to see more than a glimpse of your toes in front of your knees. Many riders make the mistake of putting their legs out in front of them in a "chair seat." This position takes your weight off your seat bones and onto your pockets. It also makes it impossible for your legs to take some of the weight and concussion.

Seat

Your seat is a valuable communication tool. With your body aligned, your two seat bones will make light contact with the saddle. Riders often make the mistake of sitting on their "pockets," which causes them to round their backs. Sitting on your seat bones makes you sit straight, and your hips can follow the motion of the horse as needed. If you're not sure where your seat bones are, lift your knees up in front of you so your thighs are parallel to the ground—this will drive your two seat bones into the saddle—then put your legs back in the correct position, maintaining soft contact with your seat bones.

As you ride, your body will move with the horse's motion, but refrain from exaggerating these movements. When you want your horse to stop or slow down, stop moving with her and increase the pressure in your seat by relaxing into the saddle. Horses are very sensitive to your seat and will begin picking up on these subtle cues.

Although it may seem impossible to maintain a correct position while being relaxed, with some practice you can achieve this desirable combination. If you feel stiffness in your heels, shoulders, hips, elbows, knees, or any other part of your body, concentrate on relaxing that part.

Practice sitting the jog and lope at home. Bouncing on your horse's back will cause her and you pain in the long run. Even if you consider yourself a western rider, master posting in the arena as well. Posting is rising up out of the saddle and sitting back down again with the motion of the horse's trot. The trot is a great, ground-covering gait and very economical, as your horse uses both sides of her body equally. Many riders also use the trot to get their

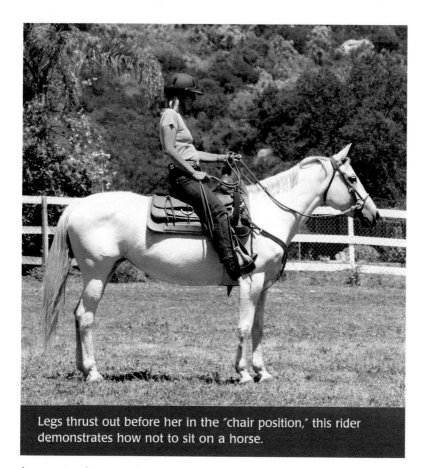

Legs thrust out before her in the "chair position," this rider demonstrates how not to sit on a horse.

horses in shape and improve their conditions. For these reasons, you may want to trot on trail when conditions permit.

The trot is a diagonal gait in which your horse's left front and right hind move together, and the right front and left hind move together. Posting requires you to rise with the horse's motion each time one of her shoulders moves forward. In a circle or arena, you will rise with your horse's outside shoulder (in an arena, this will be the shoulder closest to the fence rail), and thus be on the outside diagonal. As your chosen shoulder moves forward, your horse's natural movement will help you rise slightly up and forward out of the saddle—how far forward and up will depend on how "big" your horse's trot is. Learn to let her motion help push you up and forward, rather than pushing yourself up solely with your knees and legs. This will take practice. When posting on the trail, make sure to alternate diagonals periodically to keep from putting more pressure on one side of your horse's body than the other.

If possible, find an experienced instructor to help you learn a confident seat and practiced aids. Taking a few longe line lessons can be priceless for learning the posting trot, as the instructor will guide your horse while you focus on posting. Your horse will appreciate this, because many riders learning to post wiggle their hands and legs unintentionally. Mastering the basics in the safety of your home arena or paddock, or under the watchful eye of an instructor, will help ensure safe, enjoyable trail rides. (See chapter 1 for more information on selecting a riding instructor.)

Hands

You can ride with one rein in each hand (two handed) or with the reins in one hand, which is traditional for western riders. However, riding with a rein in each hand will give you more control over your horse's movement, so you may choose to ride two handed all the time or when your horse needs extra guidance. To hold the reins two handed, take one rein in each hand, with the rein coming from the horse's mouth, up and through the bottom of your hand. The extra rein will come out the top of your hand. Your knuckles should point forward, fingers in and thumbs facing up. Each thumb will rest on the extra rein to keep the horse from pulling the reins through your hand, and your fingers should remain loosely closed.

To turn your horse's nose, simply close your fingers tightly, as if you're squeezing out a wet sponge. Squeeze the fingers on your right hand to tip her nose right, left fingers to tip her nose left, and both hands to slow her down or ask her to stop. If this isn't enough, move your hand back an inch or two toward your hip. If you have to pull your hands all the way back to your hips to get a reaction, it's probably a sign that you are holding the reins too loosely.

If you ride single handed, with both reins in one hand, your horse will need to know how to neck rein, which means when the right rein touches her neck she turns left, and when the left rein touches her neck she turns right. One handed, you can hold the reins two different ways.

Say you choose to hold the reins in your left hand, split-rein style: The right rein will come into your fist between your pointer finger and your thumb. The left rein will be held between your pointer finger and your middle finger, and the excess of both reins

When riding two handed, cross the excess rein over and keep your thumbs up and gently resting on the excess rein, as shown here.

will fall out the bottom side of your fist. Keep your knuckles facing forward, fingers loosely closed and facing down or with the thumb slightly up.

You can also hold the reins in a loose fist, with the reins coming up from the bottom of the hand and out through the top. Hold your fingers lightly closed, thumb on top of the excess reins. If you choose to hold the reins this way, keep your thumb up, holding your hand as if you were holding an ice cream cone. Avoid twisting or tipping your hand or wrist and spilling the ice cream.

When you ride one handed, close your fingers to ask your horse to slow down or stop. You may need to move your hand toward your belly button an inch or two. To turn your horse, shift your hand gently toward her ear—right ear to turn right, left ear to turn left. Moving your hand slightly forward and to the left will lay the right rein on your horse's neck and cue her to turn left. As your hand moves toward the right ear, the left rein will cue your horse to turn right. If you're out on trail and your horse isn't responding to the neck rein, you'll have more control by taking the reins two handed and using direct pressure to guide her.

However you hold the reins—one handed, two handed, split reins—keep your hands low and near the pommel or horn. Lifting your hands too high hurts your horse's mouth and breaks the lines of communication; so do hands that venture too far out to the sides. As with your leg cues, remember to release all pressure on the reins the moment your horse responds; this is her reward.

If you're riding in a direct pressure bit, such as a snaffle, you can maintain light contact with your horse's mouth. If you're riding in a leverage bit, such as a curb bit, you don't want to exert constant pressure on your horse's mouth; however, don't hold the reins so loosely that you have to gather up a lot of rein or pull back several inches to have contact. When using a leverage bit, hold your reins so you can squeeze your fingers or move your hands only an inch or two and have contact with your horse's mouth.

When riding one handed with split reins (shown here), one rein is held between the thumb and the pointer finger and the other between the pointer finger and the middle finger. Knuckles face forward.

Whatever type of bit you choose, maintain an imaginary line from your elbow, through your arm, out your hand, and to your horse's mouth. Your elbows will be bent, with your upper arms resting gently against your body. Avoid letting your elbows come out, which will encourage your reins to flop about.

Although the eyes are not considered one of the four main aids, never underestimate the power of looking where you want to go. Your body and hands will naturally follow your eyes, even if you aren't aware of it, so keep your eyes up and forward, looking in the direction you want your horse to travel.

Voice

Voice commands will help you rely less on your reins and legs. Many horses learn commands for walk, jog/trot, lope/canter, whoa, back, and so on. Other riders use a kissing sound or a click or cluck of the tongue to cue their horses to move out. Choose a command, then pair it consistently with your other aids—seat, legs, and hands—until your horse understands what you're asking.

Mounting from the Ground

When you're out on trail, you won't have the luxury of a mounting block, and you never know when you'll need to dismount and remount. Perhaps your horse will start limping, and you'll have to get off to check her feet, or maybe there will be an obstacle in the path requiring you to dismount and move it out of the way. It's important that you can mount from both sides as well because a hillside or bushes may prevent you from mounting on the left side, which is traditional. In addition, switching the side you mount on prevents your left stirrup leather from becoming stretched and puts even wear and tear on your horse's back.

Practice mounting from the ground and on both sides in your arena or paddock first by following these steps (in this example, you are mounting from the left side):

- Take the reins in your left hand. Hold them at a length at which there's light contact with the horse's mouth but contact that allows her to move her head slightly to balance.

- Grab a handful of mane in your left hand, or simply place your left hand on your horse's neck, in front of her withers. Even though your cinch, or girth, should be snug before you mount, putting too much pressure on the saddle while you pull yourself up will likely move your saddle to the side.

- The most common position to mount from is facing the opposite direction your horse is facing. Use your right hand to hold the stirrup, and place your left foot so the ball of the

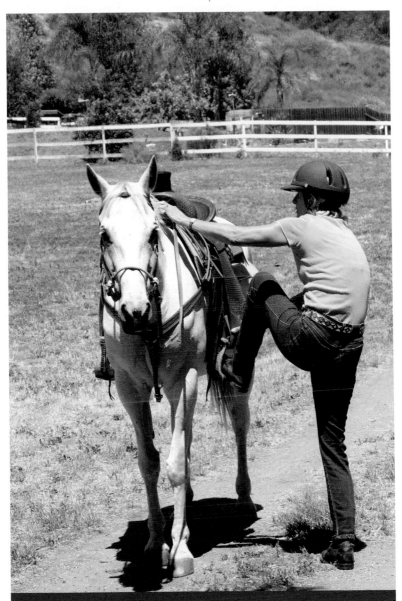

Grasping the mane so she won't pull the saddle out of place, the rider begins to mount her horse, facing toward the rear.

foot rests on the stirrup. Stay close to your horse's body while positioning your foot.

- Once your foot is in the stirrup, put your right hand on the pommel (front of the saddle, near the horn). You may need to "bounce" a little on your right foot to gain momentum, but avoid pulling on the horse or the saddle.

- Swing your right leg up and over your horse without hitting her in the flanks or on the hind end. Don't let your left toes poke into your horse's side. Lower yourself gently into the saddle.

If you simply cannot mount unassisted from the ground, you can work on strengthening your lower body, or you can try one of the various gadgets on the market. There are products available that allow you to extend your stirrup for mounting, and then bring it back into place once you're seated. A small stool you pull up with a string, fold up, and store in your saddle bag will require you to desensitize and train your horse to accept it ahead of time.

To dismount, reverse the mounting process, bringing your right leg over the horse's haunches. When your feet are even—left foot in the stirrup, right foot beside it—kick your left foot out of the stirrup and slide down. That way, if your horse walks off while you're dismounting, you won't get dragged along with your foot stuck in the stirrup or fall over.

If your horse occasionally walks off during mounting or you're out on trail and she won't hold still, try keeping the left rein, or the rein on the side you're mounting from, tighter so the horse's head is bent slightly to the left. This way, if the horse does move off unexpectedly, she'll move around you in a circle rather than walking away. However, this inhibits her ability to use her head and neck to balance. If walking off is a chronic problem, work with her in the arena.

A horse that moves every time you mount may require a helper to hold her during the first part of your retraining, or you can put her head facing the corner of your enclosure. Practice mounting, pulling back on the reins, and saying "whoa" every time your horse tries to move off. You may get only your foot in the stirrup before she moves. If so, pull back and say "whoa," trying again only once she's standing quietly. Praise her verbally and with a scratch in her favorite spot when she holds still. With patience and consistency, she'll learn that her job is to stand quietly until you're in the seat and have picked up your reins.

Riding Up and Down Hills

The rider's job is not to sit idly by while the horse does all the work! Your position in the saddle always affects how your horse moves and balances: think of how your movement and balance change when you give a child a piggyback ride. The child's movement—leaning from side to side or wiggling—affects your ability to walk. When riding uphill, help your horse by lifting your seat out of the saddle. To do this, grab a handful of mane with one or both hands midway up her neck, then lean forward and stand up slightly in your stirrups to bring your rear end a bit up and off the saddle. Make sure your reins are not pulling back on the horse's mouth as you do so.

When riding downhill, riders often mistakenly lean too far back. Instead, keep your weight centered over the horse. Although this may mean you lean your body slightly back on a very steep incline, your focus should be on keeping your weight centered. If there are trees growing on the mountainside, use them as your guide, and hold your body at the same angle as the trees. Again, don't pull back on the reins. Your horse needs enough freedom to use her neck and head to balance as she travels up- or downhill.

In general, walk up and down hills. If the footing is good and the incline not too steep, you may choose to trot up a hill as a fitness exercise for your horse. However, make sure she's up to the task, and don't let her get in the habit of speeding up every time she encounters a hill. Many horses try to trot or run up and down every hill they

As the horse moves uphill, the rider leans forward and brings her rear end slightly out of the saddle to aid her mount.

come to, but remember that you're in charge. If your horse speeds up of her own accord, take contact with her mouth, sit down in your saddle, and ask her to slow down. When she's back at the speed you want, release the pressure and resume your uphill or downhill riding position.

When faced with an extremely steep hill or one with loose footing that gives way easily, it may be advisable to dismount and walk your horse up or down the hill. Only attempt this, of course, if your horse leads well, and make her walk well to the side of you so you don't get mowed over should she begin to slide or speed up.

As the horse moves downhill, the rider keeps her weight centered over the animal. Leaning too far back can hinder your horse's movements.

Navigating Obstacles

You may encounter a number of obstacles on trail, including water crossings and fallen branches and logs. With water crossings, stay centered over your horse, giving her enough rein to navigate her course without compromising your ability to guide her as needed. If your horse has to lift her legs high to clear a log, it may help her if you assume a forward position, as you did traveling uphill—get your weight out of the saddle, and place your hand on the middle of her neck, grabbing mane if necessary.

It's always best to walk over obstacles. Unless you and your horse are experienced cross-country jumpers, jumping stationary objects, such as logs, can be extremely dangerous, as they won't give the way a jump rail in an arena would. Letting your horse run through water crossings or jump them can also be dangerous and creates a bad habit. If your horse rushes obstacles despite your attempts to slow her, practice at home (see chapter 4). While on trail, insist your horse repeat the obstacle, if safe to do so, until she walks over or through it calmly.

Riding around obstacles, such as trees, bushes, and rocks, can be another challenge. Many riders have had their legs bruised or scraped by nearby objects. The problem is your horse doesn't always realize your body sticks out and up; she'll maneuver herself safely past obstacles but forget all about your limbs! Riders often make this problem worse by turning the horse's head away from the obstacle, which actually moves the horse's body and the rider's leg closer to it. If you see your horse getting too close to something such as a tree, turn her head toward it—this will bend her body away from it, saving your leg.

If there's a tree branch hanging low over the trail, you have three options. Your first and easiest is to ride around it, but this isn't always possible. Your next choice is to bend forward over your horse's neck if it's safe to do so. The only other option is to reach forward and push the branch out of your way—either up in the air or to the side. This is when gloves come in handy. Don't attempt this unless there's no rider behind you or the rider is far enough back that you can give a warning so that no one gets slapped in the head by a branch.

You may need to ask your horse to back up on trail if the horse in front of you is backing up or if you've ridden into a tight space. Unfortunately, not all horses are taught to back up using the same cues, so make sure this is one of the skills you perfect before heading on the trail. For most horses, you will close your fingers, pulling back on the reins slightly if needed, or using a gentle give and take while squeezing with your calves or tapping if you are not getting a response.

Some horses lock up and refuse to back. If your horse does so, try "unlocking" her by using a give and take with one rein and tapping with the leg at the girth on that same side. Keep contact on the opposite rein at the same time. Although your horse may not back straight, this usually helps get her started.

Leading her horse, an equestrian takes a walking break during a group ride. On long rides, if your horse leads well, take periodic breaks.

Side-passing is another handy maneuver. This requires your horse to walk sideways without going forward. Her legs will cross over one another when she's side-passing correctly. You can use this maneuver to get your horse close to an object, such as a gate you need to open. Keep gentle contact on the reins to hold your horse relatively straight and keep her from going forward. It may be helpful to tip her nose slightly in the opposite direction you're asking her to move. One of your legs will ask your horse to move over. For example, use your left leg to ask your horse to right. Squeeze with your calf at the girth, tapping if she needs more motivation. If she moves her shoulder over more than her hip, you can bring your leg farther back to move her hind end over. At first, ask only for a step or two in each direction until you and your horse master the maneuver. Practice side-passing at home in the open first.

Loosening Up with Stretches

Although proper equitation will help keep you comfortable in the saddle, long rides are bound to make even the best rider a bit stiff. Dismounting and walking your horse for a few minutes when it's safe to do so can be a huge help. If your horse is calm and you're on a flat trail with few distractions, you can stop and perform some in-the-saddle stretches. Try these stretches at home in the safety of your paddock or arena before you attempt them on trail, as your strange movements may startle your horse.

The goal of these stretches and any others you find helpful is to change positions and give your stiff joints and muscles a break from the traditional riding position. The leg and toe stretches will require you to take your feet out of the stirrups. (See pages 82–85.)

Stretch 1: Take one foot out of the stirrup, and stretch your toe down toward the ground as far as you can (A). Hold this position for a few moments, and then stretch your toes up toward the sky as high as you can (B). Switch between toes up and toes down for several repetitions.

Stretch 2: Point your toes toward your horse's front feet, leg stretched straight, and hold them there for a few moments (A). Next, point your toes back toward your horse's hind feet, which will require you to bring your lower leg slightly back, too (B). Be careful not to bump your horse's sensitive flanks. Switch between the two positions several times.

Stretch 3: Draw a slow circle with your toes—as large as you can, first in one direction, then in the other, keeping your legs still.

Stretch 4: With your feet in the stirrups, rotate your back and shoulders so that you're facing to the right, keeping your seat in the saddle and your hips pointing forward. Put your right hand on the cantle, or back of your seat, and keep the reins in your left hand near the horn. Hold this position for a few moments, then switch and face to the left. Repeat several times. This exercise stretches your back.

Stretch 5: Practice standing up in the saddle—at a standstill or a walk—to stretch your legs and give you a break from sitting. You can also "practice" this stretch when your horse stops to urinate to get your weight off her back and make it easier for her. Hold the horn or mane if you need to steady yourself.

Stretch 6: With your reins held loosely and your hands even and near the front of the saddle, squeeze your shoulder blades together, stretching your chest and relieving tension in your shoulders. Hold for a few seconds and repeat.

Stretch 7: Maintaining the same hand position as above, squeeze your shoulders up toward your ears, relieving the pressure in the muscles between your shoulders and neck. Hold for a several seconds, and then pull your shoulders down toward the ground. Hold and repeat.

If any of the stretches cause you discomfort, or you have a medical problem, do not perform them without consulting your doctor.

Practicing proper riding position and techniques will pay off in added comfort for you and your horse and a more responsive horse that understands what you're asking.

Above: Stretch 1A   Below: Stretch 1B

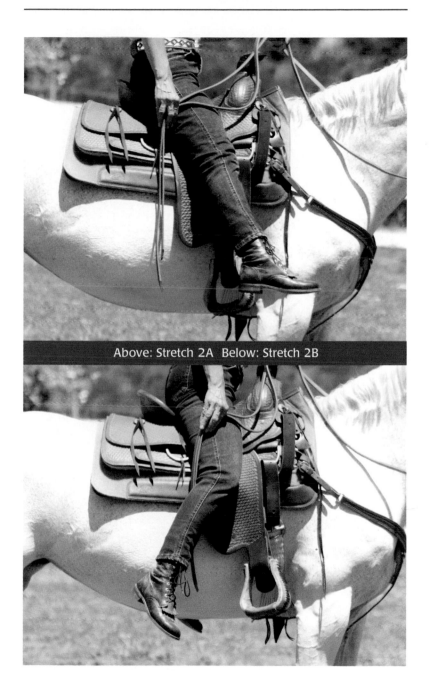

Above: Stretch 2A   Below: Stretch 2B

Stretch 4

Stretch 5

Desensitization

Trail riding is by nature unpredictable. You never know what you may encounter as you head down your street to the local trails or into a state park. Chances are you'll see lawn mowers, weed whackers, leaf blowers, motorcycles, strollers, bicycles, and skateboards. You may even pass by a child's birthday party, complete with balloons, party streamers, and noisemakers. When you come across situations, objects, and activities such as these, it helps to know how your horse might react. If you've done your homework, your horse will probably walk calmly by with not much more than a glance.

The homework involved is the process of desensitization. Police horses go through intensive desensitization so they'll remain calm and responsive no matter what they encounter on city streets or during crowd control. The more situations, objects, activities, vehicles, and animals you can expose your horse to in a safe and controlled environment, the better your chances are that he'll react calmly when you encounter strange sights and sounds on your local streets or out on the trail.

Before Beginning

Before you attempt any desensitization work with your horse, make sure he leads without crowding, pushing, or pulling you and that he's responsive under saddle in an arena or a paddock—that is, he will walk, jog, lope, stop, back up, stand still, and side-pass when requested. In addition, you'll need a flat, enclosed area with good footing and safe fencing.

You'll also need to be a confident leader. If your horse scares you or you feel timid working around him when he's nervous, hire an experienced trainer, and do not try desensitization with your horse on your own.

You'll need to become adept at reading your horse's signals as well. Desensitization work means your horse will be pushed slightly out of his comfort zone but not to the point at which he's completely frightened and incapable of learning. For example, a horse that's a little nervous will look at the new object with ears forward, head up. He may even snort or fidget. If you push him beyond that point by trying to move closer or adding elements before he's ready, he may try to spin or bolt or run around you on the lead line, and one or both of you may get hurt.

Your horse shouldn't be the only one getting ready for trail during these training sessions. You should practice staying calm, cool, and collected. Remember that horses are very sensitive. If one herd member is afraid, all members will take notice. As the leader of your "herd," you must remain calm when your horse is nervous. Practice this during your desensitization work with him at home. Breathe deeply and relax. Even such subtle actions as holding your breath or tensing up will signal your horse that you're nervous.

Trail Gear

Start with the items and actions you'll use on trail. For example, your horse will need to accept any saddlebags, water bottles, or canteens and collapsible buckets you plan to attach to his saddle for a ride. Once he accepts these items on his saddle, he'll need to accept their being removed and used. You may also plan to tie or pack a jacket or a parka. He must to get used to this as well as your putting the jacket on while mounted. Any time you add an element or piece of equipment, accustom your horse to the change at home first.

In preparation for a trail ride, saddlebags and a jacket have been attached to the saddle. Desensitize your horse to such items ahead of time.

Let him smell the new object, then move it around so he can hear any sounds it makes and see it from all angles. Next, touch him with the object, such as your saddlebag or jacket, while you pet him and speak to him reassuringly. When he's comfortable with this, put the item where it will be during your ride. If he seems calm, attach it and walk him around, then jog so that he gets used to the feeling of it there and any sound it makes. Once your horse has completely accepted the object from the ground, you can mount up in your safe area and ride him with the item in place. Last, use the item while mounted, such as opening your saddlebag and removing something or untying your jacket to put it on. Don't progress further than your horse is comfortable. Perform multiple lessons if necessary.

A rider walks her Paint Horse through the gate she's set up in the arena to get him used to performing that task on trail.

Trail Obstacles

At horse shows, trail classes test a horse's skills in trail navigating situations. Trail classes often ask horses to walk over wooden bridges on the ground; stand still while you open gates and pass through; and step over, back through, or side-pass over ground poles. All of these maneuvers demonstrate a horse's trail skills because they deal with obstacles you may encounter on an actual trail ride. Re-create these challenges at home in your arena or paddock. They will build your relationship with your horse, improve his responsiveness and your ability to accurately cue him, and prepare you both for challenges you may come across on trail. Before you approach the obstacles mounted, get your horse used to them from the ground. Once your horse handles trail course obstacles well from the ground, you can ride him through the course. It may take some practice to fine-tune your cues so you can back your horse in a straight line or side-pass him without his walking forward or backward or letting his hips or shoulders fall out of line. This will come in handy when you're out on trail and want to open a gate without dismounting,

An Arabian begins walking across a board, meant to simulate the sound and the feel of a bridge a horse and rider might encounter on trail.

cross a country bridge safely, or move backward or sideways out of a tight spot.

Ground Poles

Start simply with the ground poles. These are rounded boards several inches in diameter and several feet long. Pick solid boards in good condition. Let your horse smell one, then ask him to walk over it. Eventually, you can add poles. At first, place them about two feet apart or at a distance your horse can comfortably walk through, which will be determined by his size and length of stride. After that becomes easy, vary the distance so he has to think about it and walk carefully. Next, take a single ground pole and raise it a few inches on one side by setting it up on a block of wood. Ask your horse to walk over the raised pole, as he may have to walk over fallen branches or other objects on the trail. Then raise both sides a few inches. Painting the ground poles different colors will also help desensitize your horse to walking over various objects you may encounter on the trail.

When he's comfortable walking over ground poles, you can even side-pass him over a pole or ask him to back between two. Of course, he must perform these maneuvers easily without any obstacles first. Backing up and side-passing, where your horse walks sideways with his legs crossing, will certainly be useful at some point in your trail career. You want to know you have complete control over where your horse puts his legs and body and can direct him as needed.

If you have access to other types of trail obstacles, such as gates, let your horse smell them, then open and shut them so he's comfortable with the sounds and movements. Praise him for his bravery with kind words and a little scratch.

Foreign Footing

Bridges can be tricky for horses that aren't used to them, so it may take some time to accustom him to it. Make sure the bridge you use is sturdy enough to handle the weight of a horse. Most trail course bridges are several inches off the ground and a few feet wide and long, but you can also make one by laying a board flat on the ground. Lead your horse up to the bridge enough times that he's completely relaxed approaching and smelling it. Stand on the bridge yourself a few times. Next, step up on the bridge, and ask your horse to walk with you. If he's scared, he may get only one foot on it the first day; if so, praise him and move on to something else. With time and patience, your horse will walk quietly over the bridge with you.

Whenever you're asking your horse to pass over a new obstacle, watch out—he may decide to run or jump over it. Always keep your eyes on him, and keep yourself in a safe position. Watch his body language as well. If he's nervous approaching the obstacle, it's a good indication he may run or jump over it, so step to the side, well out of his way.

You can use the same process to ask your horse to walk over other safe obstacles, such as a burlap sack or tarp. With these soft items, you can fold them so that at first they're small and he can easily step over them. Over days or weeks, you can slowly unfold them until he's comfortable first putting a foot on them and eventually walking over them. There are many things your horse will have to walk over on the trail, including water, cement and pavement, dry leaves, wooden bridges, mud, and small branches, so teaching him to walk willingly over footing that feels different or makes noise will prepare him and help him trust your judgment and leadership.

Scary Objects

Introducing your horse to objects he may see on trail in the safety and comfort of your stable can save you from a lot of spooks. Be creative, but always keep safety in mind. Never introduce your horse to anything that could hurt him or that he could become entangled in or attached to. In addition, always monitor your horse's fear level. If

Hang some flags, a clothesline, or streamers at a safe distance from your horse's pen. When he's comfortable with them, walk him closer.

he's a little nervous but still curious and responsive, you're in the right zone: you've pushed him out of his comfort level but not into a state of panic. If your horse becomes extremely afraid or agitated or starts to panic, he will not be able to learn, and the training will actually be detrimental. Desensitization takes time. You can introduce one new object every day as part of your routine.

With every object, the goal is to get your horse to touch it with his nose, and when he's comfortable with the object in a stationary position, to move it or rattle it or change its position. Start with something common, such as a plastic grocery bag. Most horses are scared of plastic bags to one extent or another, and it is likely you'll encounter a wayward bag along the road or trail at some point. Tie the plastic bag by its handles to a fence post in your arena or paddock area. This way the bag can still billow and move but will not blow around out of control.

Walk your horse in large circles in both directions, circling closer and closer to the bag as his comfort level increases. If he gets nervous several feet or even yards from it, move your circle farther away. You can also occasionally let your horse stop and look at the object. Circling can be more effective than walking straight toward the scary object. Walking straight at it puts your focus and your horse's focus on it. Circling gives him something to do and helps teach him that new objects are a normal part of his environment—nothing to get worked up about. Circling and spiraling in also allow him to see the object from all angles.

Once your horse has looked at the bag and circled past it many times in close proximity, casually walk up to the bag. Again, watch his comfort level. If he's still uncomfortable, walk him in a few more circles, or ask him to back or side-pass to get his mind off the bag and focused on you. Then try moving closer to the bag. Remember to praise him for any progress. You may be able to walk right up to the bag and let the horse touch his nose to it and sniff it, or you may have to be satisfied with staying twenty feet away that first day. It all depends on your horse. You may even choose to stash a few pieces of carrot or horse cookies in the bag. If your horse is comfortable, you can reach in and pull one out for him. When your horse is calmly approaching the bag and doesn't mind when you shake or move the bag, it's time to move on to another sensory item.

Strollers are another item that can scare horses. Use the same technique as with the bag, but this time place the stroller in the middle of your arena. Start with large circles in both directions. When you've reached the distance where your horse won't go closer, stay at that distance from the stroller (or other sensory item), spiraling in only as your horse gains confidence.

When your horse is calmly walking up to the stroller and smelling it, try rolling the stroller away from the horse (never toward him). Horses will be less intimidated by an object that moves away

At liberty, an Arabian examines objects in the pen. Place new objects in the pen only after your horse is first comfortable with them outside it.

from them—something a predator wouldn't do. You can even add a baby doll or stuffed animal inside the stroller once he's comfortable with the stroller alone. Think of other objects you may see on your rides, such as bouncing balls and umbrellas, and continue your training sessions. Be creative. Don't limit yourself to objects. Draw a line in the dirt with chalk—it will look like the lines in the road, which believe it or not can scare a horse. You may see chalk lines on trail if a cross-country run has been held there or at a horse show for a keyhole race.

Always introduce the items to your horse on the ground. Once he's comfortable, you can saddle up and get on because often a horse is less brave with the rider on his back. Keep your desensitization sessions short, and always end on a positive note, even if that means calmly circling several yards away from the object.

Placing items near your horse's corral or paddock is another way to desensitize him and teach him new sights are part of his

Having desensitized his Hanoverian mare to various items on a lead line, the rider now approaches them in the saddle.

everyday life. In fact, it's easier on you and often less stressful to your horse. You can combine this method with the in-hand method, first introducing the items near your horse's pen, then placing them inside the arena.

Put up a flag near his corral or pasture, or tie some balloons. Hang a clothesline, complete with flapping tarp.

One caveat: don't move items too close to your horse's living quarters too quickly. If your horse is scared, he may not go near his water bucket or feed, or he may hurt himself trying to escape. Place the object 40 or 50 feet away at first; if your horse is comfortable with it from that distance, move it a bit closer every day until it's attached to or near his actual pen. Don't put anything within his reach that could harm him, of course.

Water Crossings

Crossing water can be a trail rider's biggest challenge. Many horses resist water crossing because it's foreign to them—they don't know how deep it is or what lies beneath. If you already know your horse crosses water easily, you're in luck and don't need to practice at home. However, if your horse is afraid to cross water, start small. Turn the garden hose tap on low, and let it run in an area around your stable to create a ministream. As with your other desensitiza-tion work, lead your horse up to the "stream." Take him as close as you can without pushing him too far out of his comfort zone. You should be able to walk him up to the running stream, let him look at it up close and smell it your first day.

If he's not too frightened, stand in the stream and encourage him to walk over. Most likely, he'll jump the first time, so stay out of his way. Praise him when he gets to the other side, then turn around and try it again. Continue crossing until he walks through and doesn't jump over the water. Eventually you may have to take the hose and "widen" the stream so your horse has to walk through the water instead of jumping it.

With a reassuring pat, a rider encourages her Paint Horse to cross the artificial stream created by a friend with a hose.

After he's easily crossing the hose stream, make a deeper and wider puddle somewhere. Use the same steps as before until your horse is walking through the puddle. Be patient: this may take several days or weeks if your horse has a major aversion to crossing water. Always praise even the smallest effort, such as one hoof placed in the water.

When it's time to actually cross water on trail, choose a narrow, shallow crossing free of rocks or other dangerous debris. Take along an experienced lead horse that will cross willingly, and don't be in a hurry. You may only be able to get him up to the water to smell it the first day, so be prepared to follow the same steps as above until he's confident enough to cross. Never force your horse across water; he'll only fear the experience even more the next time, and force puts both of you in danger. When exposed to enough water crossings over time—and with a great deal of patience—your horse will learn to navigate water confidently.

A Texan and his buckskin Quarter Horse gelding splash through the shallows of a stream. When crossing water, choose the shallowest (often the widest) part.

Whenever you cross streams or rivers, look for the best crossing point. Usually the widest parts are the shallowest, and therefore the best, choices. Avoid crossings that require you to ride down a steep incline to get to the water or crossings full of rocks or sharp branches.

If the water in a stream is potable, let your horse enjoy a good long drink at every opportunity. This will be important when you take longer rides and need your horse to stay hydrated. But be wary if he starts to paw and play in the water: he may be preparing to take a roll! In this case, turn his head toward the bank, and push him forward with your legs.

Mud can be another problem. You may encounter it near streams or on the trail itself after a rain. (*Always* avoid bogs or deep mud.) Desensitize your horse to shallow mud at home. The hose "stream" you made at home to teach your horse to cross water can also be used to teach him to go through mud. Turn the hose off, and follow the same process you used to get him to cross water. An easier way is to create a bit of mud in his corral, such as around his water trough. Just keep the manure picked up, and keep the rest of his corral dry.

Animals, Activities, and Vehicles

Moving objects—such as animals, humans, and vehicles—usually scare horses more than the stationary objects covered in the previous sections. Because horses are prey, animals, humans, and vehicles may appear as predators to them. However, using desensitization methods, you can help teach your horse that other domesticated animals, humans at play, and vehicles are not a threat.

Other Animals

Farm animals—including cattle, sheep, goats, and llamas—can frighten horses that aren't used to them. They smell, sound, and move differently than horses do. For this reason, exposing your horse to as many farm animals as you can in a safe environment is an excellent idea. If you're lucky enough to keep your horse somewhere with a variety of other livestock, you're one step ahead of the game. There's nothing better to get a horse used to other animals than living near them. Your next best option is friendly neighbors who may have barnyard animals you can expose your horse to in a safe environment.

Desensitize your horse to other farm animals in the same way you did to objects in the area, except in this case you'll need to lead your horse to the other animal's pen. Go only as close as your horse is comfortable the first day, then circle and walk around at that distance. Your horse will see the other animals moving around, maybe even making some noises. Hang around at that distance for a bit, then try going a tad closer, or call it a day and return the next day.

Dogs can be a problem for trail horses as well. Bringing dogs who are used to horses around the barn is the easiest way to get horses used to them. If your barn doesn't already have a "barn dog," borrow a horse-safe dog from a friend to bring to your stable. Leash the dog, and let the dog and handler hang out near the horse's corral, getting closer as the horse's comfort level increases.

Human Activities

Run a lawn mower and leaf blower from a safe distance. Get creative: ask a few friends to play football, toss a large beach ball back and forth outside your horse's pen, or bounce a basketball near his corral. Even hiking attire may spook your horse, so play dress-up! Put on different hats, a raincoat, and a backpack, or carry a walking stick. Remember to start out far away, and move closer only as your horse's tolerance increases.

Some people also tout the value of noise desensitization—for example, playing a CD or a tape of people clapping, loud music, or vehicles. There are CDs especially for desensitizing horses. If you use this method, keep the sessions short, and remember that horses have sensitive ears, so don't overdo the volume. Again, watch his comfort level, and don't push him too far past his comfort zone.

Moving Vehicles

To reach many trails these days, you'll have to ride along a road or a parking lot for at least a short distance. Cars, motorcycles, bicycles, and skateboards all can scare horses. A horse that panics around traffic is extremely dangerous. If you're not 100 percent sure how your horse handles traffic—including motorcycles, bikes, and skateboards—or you know he could use some improvement, desensitize him to vehicles and test his comfort level before riding on or near roadways.

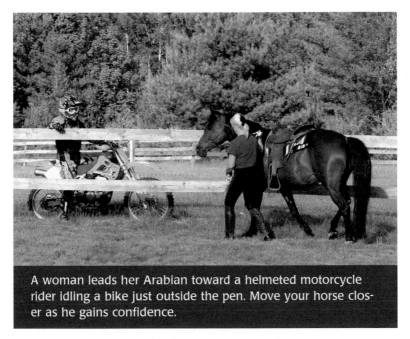

A woman leads her Arabian toward a helmeted motorcycle rider idling a bike just outside the pen. Move your horse closer as he gains confidence.

The easiest way to do this is to turn your horse out in an arena or a paddock (that's safely fenced) near a road. This way, your horse can get used to the sights and sounds of various vehicles passing by. Of course, you'll first need to walk your horse around the area so he knows its boundaries, and make sure he's not overly panicked about being close to a road. If he's getting worked up while you lead him, it's a sign you need to start farther away—perhaps another pasture over—or simply lead him around at a distance from the road where he's still somewhat comfortable.

If a safe paddock or arena near a road is not available, ask a friend to drive a car down the drive and into your stable area. This won't bother most horses but can still provide useful lessons. Stand on the other side of a fence with your horse, and watch the car drive back and forth, or stand or circle your horse from 40 to 60 feet away. Most horses will be used to the occasional car. Once your horse is comfortable watching the car drive back and forth, have your friend stop and rev the engine, then drive on. Assure your horse with praise and a scratch that all is well. If he gets antsy and starts to wiggle, ask him to walk in a circle or move farther away for a few minutes. When your horse doesn't mind the engine revving, ask your friend to mimic other things drivers may do, such as beep the horn, wave, shout, whistle, and slam the door. Have a brief conversation with your friend in the car. After your horse is calm for all of this on the ground, progress to under saddle work while your friend repeats the steps. This same process can be done with bicycles, skateboards, motorcycles, and lawn mowers. You can also let your horse approach these items and smell them. Remember to keep sessions short and take your time. Twenty minutes is plenty.

A road is a different beast than a single car, of course. Your first experience riding near a road with a new horse or a horse you haven't ridden in traffic needs to be carefully planned. Pick a trail or paddock area that's within the sight and sound of the road but far enough away that if your horse becomes frightened, there's no danger of him bolting or spooking out in front of the cars. Keep riding at this safe distance until your horse is completely comfortable walking near traffic.

Avoid riding very close to roads whenever possible. It is always somewhat dangerous, even on the calmest horse. If your horse does become nervous and antsy near a road, try to move him away from traffic, even if that means going off the trail. If that's not an option and you can safely dismount, you may choose to do so. When horses get upset, they sometimes dance and fidget or bolt toward traffic. A panicked rider sometimes kicks and pulls back on the reins, giving the horse nowhere to go. Always give your horse a place to go and something to do when he's nervous. Try to move him forward down the trail or away from the road by encouraging him with your legs and gently guiding his nose in the direction you want him to go. Horses move away from pressure, so use your leg closest to the road to push him away from the traffic. If your horse tries to

In Manvers, Ontario, two riders travel single file down the road, keeping to the right-hand side, the direction of traffic.

back rapidly into the street, turn him to face it instead. This way he can see the traffic, and if he's panicking and backing is his chosen mode, you can back him away from the street.

Never ride on busy streets until you know your horse will remain calm and responsive, and avoid going on group rides near roads unless all the horses in the group are known to be safe in traffic. When you do ride on roads, think safety first and follow traffic laws, including riding with the direction of traffic and using crosswalks whenever possible. Always wear bright clothing when riding on or near streets. If you must cross the street in an unmarked area, signal approaching drivers to slow down or stop.

Familiarize yourself with local and state laws regarding horses and roads. Some states offer certain protection to horses, such as prohibiting cars from passing them, whereas others restrict where a horse can ride, including along road shoulders or in medians.

Never ride faster than a walk on pavement or cement. Not only is it too hard on your horse's feet and legs, it can be very dangerous, as pavement and cement are slippery for horses. Barefoot horses often have better traction than shod horses but less protection. If you have to ride on pavement or cement regularly, talk to your farrier about the best protection for your horse.

Many motorists are oblivious to the needs of horses and won't slow down on their own. They may even beep their horn in what they perceive as a friendly "hello," so you must ride defensively.

Off-road motorcycles and ATVs can be another problem. Ask a friend to help you desensitize your horse to these at home as described above. Many state and national parks have restrictions that limit where off-road motorcycles and ATVs can ride, but if you ride in areas not maintained and regulated by a park authority, you may end up sharing the trails with motorized vehicles. These bikes can be much louder than street bikes. If you hear one coming, try to take a different route. If a bike approaches, hold up your hand to signal him to slow down, and move off the trail as much as you can. Polite bikers will slow down as they pass or stop and let you pass. Always thank them for this courtesy.

Time Well Spent

All this desensitization may seem like a lot of work, but it's time well spent. Most horses have one thing or another that scares them, so even if your horse is more or less "bombproof," work on the areas he needs improvement on and skip the things he already has down pat. Neither the horse nor the rider enjoys a trail ride full of spooks and anxiety. With just a little time each day, you can build upon your horse's strengths and overcome his weaknesses.

Here a group of calm, well-behaved horses enjoy a pleasant trail ride.

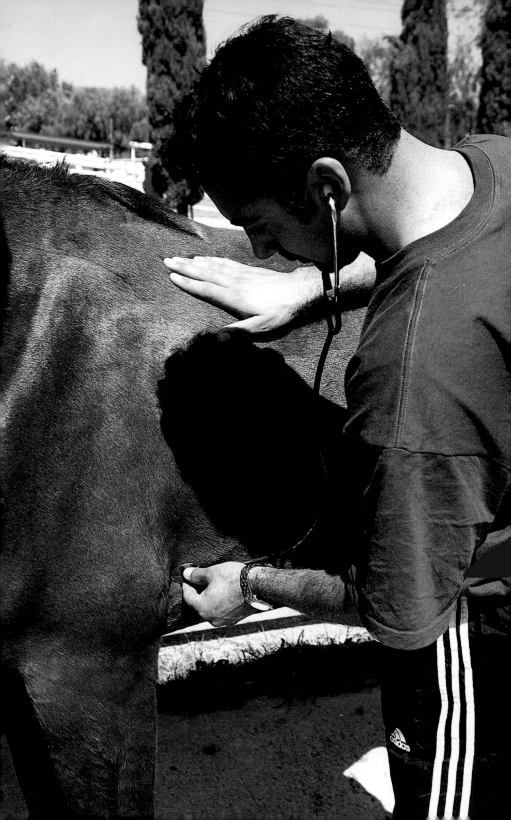

Proper Planning

The old motto "better to be safe than sorry" applies any time you're dealing with horses and doubly so when you're heading out on trail and will be far from home. There are many steps you can take to ensure your and your horse's safety and comfort on the trail.

Preventive Maintenance

Regular veterinary and farrier care are inexpensive compared with emergency treatment or replacement of a good horse.

Veterinary Care

At the very least, a veterinarian should see your trail horse twice a year for vaccinations and a dental checkup. Depending on your area, where you keep your horse, and where you take her, she may need boosters more often. Your veterinarian can help you devise an appropriate vaccination schedule. Horses generally need their teeth floated, or filed, once a year. If sharp points or other problems develop, your horse won't be able to chew her food properly, which can cause weight loss and other health issues. Teeth problems can also cause her to misbehave under saddle; she may resent bridling or toss her head when ridden. Keeping up with your horse's veterinary care will ensure she has a longer, more enjoyable, and useful life.

Farrier Care

Horses need to see a farrier every six to eight weeks to have their feet trimmed or new shoes put on. You have three choices when it comes

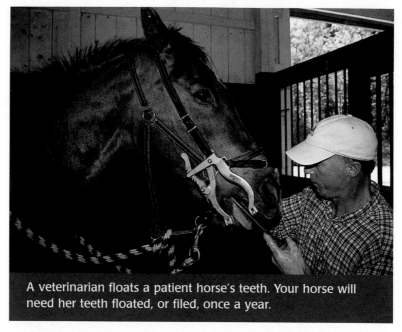

A veterinarian floats a patient horse's teeth. Your horse will need her teeth floated, or filed, once a year.

to your horse's feet, and your farrier can help you determine which is right for your horse: She can go barefoot all the time; she can go barefoot but wear removable hoof boots, similar to tennis shoes for horses, when you ride on rough terrain; or she can wear horseshoes on the front feet or all four feet. Not every horse can go barefoot. Some have especially weak or sensitive feet and will need shoes. Others have soundness or conformation problems that corrective shoeing can help. If you plan to take part in organized or competitive rides, these may require shoes, so do your research. The type of terrain you ride over also may dictate whether your horse can go barefoot. Find a farrier you trust, and work with him or her to find the best option for your horse.

If you live in an icy or snowy region and you plan to ride during the winter, discuss the options with your farrier based on your horse's needs and your winter riding goals. There are a number of shoeing choices that can help your horse gain better traction in icy conditions, including studs (or calks), which are like cleats for your horse, or a material called borium, which your farrier can add to your horse's shoes to improve her traction. Shod horses can wear snow pads to keep snow from balling up in the hooves. Spraying the bottom of a horse's hooves with cooking oil also can help prevent the snow from sticking and packing in, but that is only a temporary fix.

Never go riding if your horse has a loose shoe. Call the farrier and wait until he can come to fix it. The same applies to hooves that are too long, cracking, or otherwise in poor condition. Trail riding can be hard on hooves, so don't attempt it unless your horse's hooves have been attended to and are in good condition.

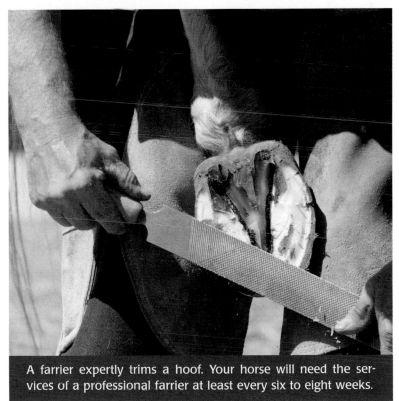

A farrier expertly trims a hoof. Your horse will need the services of a professional farrier at least every six to eight weeks.

Tack Care

Your tack also needs preventive maintenance. Clean and condition your leather regularly, and wash all nylon, cotton, and synthetic items as needed. Each time you use your tack, inspect it for wear and tear. Replace anything that's starting to become thin, cracked, or damaged.

Preventive Grooming

Start every ride with a good grooming. Cleaning your horse ensures that nothing is under the tack that could irritate her. In addition, it keeps her skin and coat healthy and is the perfect opportunity for giving her a thorough once-over.

A Thorough Once-Over

Does your horse have any areas where her skin is scabby, irritated, or losing hair? This could be a sign of a skin condition, such as a fungus. When you curry over her back, does she flinch or hollow her back? If so, it could indicate back pain caused by poor saddle fit or other issues. When you groom your horse's chest and head, are there bare spots that show the bridle or breast collar may not fit correctly and may be rubbing? As you brush her legs, do you notice any swellings, lumps, or bumps? These could indicate a minor injury or a more serious condition, especially if the area is hot or sore. If you feel or see something on one leg, compare it with the other leg to determine what is out of the ordinary. Always call your veterinarian if there's any problem. Your veterinarian will tell you how to proceed.

Hoof Care

A thorough grooming also includes picking out each of your horse's hooves before and after every ride. This will remove manure and mud, which can lead to destructive conditions such as thrush. Picking the hooves will also remove debris that can cause stone bruises and other problems. If you notice a problem with your horse's hooves or shoes, discuss it with your farrier.

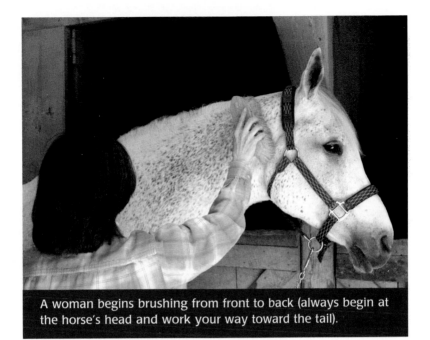

A woman begins brushing from front to back (always begin at the horse's head and work your way toward the tail).

Repelling Insects

Flies and mosquitoes can pose a problem from the late spring through early fall. After a thorough grooming, spray or wipe on fly repellent until your horse's coat is slightly damp. You'll also need to treat your horse's head and ears with a roll-on fly repellent or liquid repellent applied to a rag. You may want to pack fly-repellent towelettes or a rag soaked in fly spray in a resealable bag for reapplication on long rides. Biting insects are not only irritating but also pose a safety hazard if your horse becomes bothered enough!

When fly repellents aren't enough, you may want to add a barrier, such as a crocheted ear bonnet, to keep biting insects out of your horse's ears and away from her forehead and eyes. There are also mesh fly masks available for riding that do not obstruct your horse's vision. Don't forget to protect yourself. Apply insecticide to exposed skin, or wear a light long-sleeved shirt.

A crocheted ear bonnet protects this Tennessee Walking Horse mare from the annoyance and danger of biting insects in Ontario's Ganaraska Forest.

Ticks can also be a problem for horses and humans. If you ride in areas where ticks are common, check yourself and your horse when you return from a ride. The best way to remove a tick is with a sharp tweezers or commercially made tick remover. Make sure to pull the tick out by the head so that no piece is left embedded in the skin.

Conditioning

You wouldn't attempt an all-day hike uphill if your normal exercise routine consisted of walking to the mailbox, right? If you made it at all, you would no doubt feel awful the next day; you might even injure yourself. Just like humans, horses must build condition over time. They are not ATVs that can be taken out for an all-day joyride every once in a while.

Don't ask your horse to do more than she's conditioned to do. Some trail riders are "weekend warriors," taking their horses out for trail rides only on the weekends. If you ride only on the weekends, you'll need to keep your rides very short and easy, and make sure your horse lives in a pasture or has a daily turnout during the week. Your other option is to find another rider or a horse trainer who can help you exercise your horse during the week.

Talk to a Veterinarian

Before starting any conditioning program, talk to your veterinarian. Your veterinarian can help you decide if your horse is physically up to the tasks you have planned and can offer advice specific to your horse's needs. Remember as well that after a long winter off or other layup, you'll need to start back to work very slowly. In addition, make sure your horse is a proper weight before you begin a conditioning program. An underweight horse won't have the fat stores to burn during a workout, and an overweight horse will tire quickly and be more apt to overheat. Your veterinarian can help you determine the best diet for your horse based on her health and workload. The more calories a horse burns, the more calories she must eat, so you may need to adjust her diet as you increase her workload.

Horses need salt and minerals in their diet. Once you and your veterinarian come up with the ideal nutrition plan for your horse, ask your veterinarian about the best way for your horse to get the salt and minerals she needs. Depending on your horse's exercise routine and her diet, your veterinarian may recommend offering your horse loose salt or a salt block or adding electrolytes to your horse's diet. Always consult your veterinarian before starting your horse on any nutritional supplement.

Commonsense Program

The old rule of thumb for humans—exercise at least three days a week—also holds true of horses. Any less, and they won't be in shape for more than a stroll down the lane. However, like people, most horses will benefit from one or two days off per week to relax and enjoy their pasture or some turnout.

A commonsense approach to fitness works for most pleasure trail riders. If you want to take faster, longer, or steeper rides, add speed, length, and hills to your horse's workouts slowly over several months. However, never add more than one element at a time. For example, add a bit of hill work or some faster work, or make your rides a bit longer, but never all three or even two at once. Adding a bit of long trotting is great way to build a horse's condition for faster rides; just make sure you do so on appropriate footing (no holes, rocks, or pavement). Long trotting is basically a fast and ground-covering or extended trot. For example, during your rides you may long trot your horse for five minutes three to six days a week for a couple of weeks, and then move it up to 10 minutes. Riding up hills is also a good way to build muscle on your horse or prepare her for steeper rides. Again, start with mild to moderate short inclines for several weeks before adding steeper or longer climbs. Adding 10 or so minutes each week to your rides will improve your horse's endurance for longer rides.

Watch your horse's breathing and sweating to note when she's getting fatigued, but keep in mind that these are also affected by weather. Your horse will sweat more and breathe more heavily on hotter days. Use common sense, and put yourself in your horse's shoes to make logical judgments about her fitness regimen.

To improve the horse's condition for difficult trails, this rider takes her horse up a steep incline.

Heart Monitor

If you're preparing for long-distance competition, such as endurance or competitive trail riding, you'll need to take a more systematic approach to conditioning. Find an experienced mentor to help you along the way. See the Resources section for information on how to contact the endurance and competitive trail associations. These groups will help match you with an experienced mentor. This person, along with your veterinarian, can help you plan your conditioning program. You will need to begin your horse's fitness program a year or so in advance of your first long-distance ride.

Before you begin to seriously condition your horse for long-distance riding, you'll need to invest in an equine heart-rate monitor or learn to check her pulse and heart rate by hand. This will help you determine how much your horse can handle during each phase of her conditioning. An average horse's resting heart rate or pulse is 30 to 42 beats per minute. In general, the quicker your horse's heart rate returns to normal (at rest) after exertion, the better shape she's in. In addition to checking your horse's heart after exertion, a heart-rate monitor allows you to monitor her heart rate during a workout to determine when she is in her target zone; when she can be pushed farther, faster, or longer; and when you should back off.

Monitoring your horse's heart rate will give you a much more accurate measurement of her fitness and exertion, but keep in mind that even dismounting to take her pulse will allow enough time for her heart rate to drop slightly, which is why many serious long-distance riders purchase a heart-rate monitor.

Rider Fitness

Don't overlook your own fitness. An unfit rider becomes merely a passenger—dead weight—rather than a partner, making the horse's job much harder. Fit riders can easily post the trot for long distances and can take their weight out of the saddle for hill work, in addition to maintaining proper form throughout the ride. Aerobic exercise such as running, biking, brisk walking, and swimming will improve your stamina. Strength training, including weight lifting and resistance exercises such as lunges and squats will improve your muscle tone and strength. Stretching, Pilates, and yoga promote flexibility. Virtually any exercise that increases your fitness can make you a better, more capable, and more comfortable rider. Fitness also helps you avoid aches, pains, and injuries such as muscle and tendon pulls. You and your horse will appreciate your fitness on long rides!

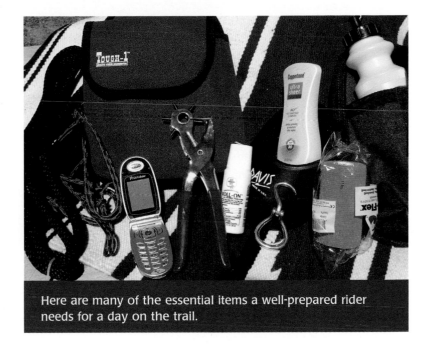

Here are many of the essential items a well-prepared rider needs for a day on the trail.

Packing for the Trail

There are certain essentials some trail riders overlook. Even if you ride for only an hour or two at a time, purchase at least a small saddle horn or cantle bag to carry a few supplies in.

What to Bring

Never leave the following items at home:

Cell phone: Place it in a holder on your belt, leg, or arm or in a fanny pack. Avoid storing it in your saddlebag in case you and your horse are separated by a fall or other accident. Program in phone numbers for your family and your veterinarian.

Identification: Place your name and an emergency contact number somewhere on yourself and your horse in case the two of you become separated. You can get a dog tag made and attach it to your saddlebags or your horse's tack. For yourself, always carry at least a piece of paper with your name, address, phone number, an emergency contact, and your veterinarian's number. Fold it and store it in your pocket. In the unlikely event you're knocked unconscious, someone will be able to identify you and call for help. If you have any medical conditions, such as diabetes, wear a medical bracelet or include this information on the above piece of paper.

First aid kit for your horse: You may also choose to include a first aid kit for yourself, but many of the items in your horse's first aid kit could be used on a human, and you can throw in a few Band-Aids for good measure. A basic horse first aid kit should include at least: small scissors, gauze, self-adhesive vet tape, nonstick pads or wrap, antiseptic or antibiotic solution, and a thermometer.

Hoof boot: If your horse is shod, pack a hoof boot in case she loses a shoe in the middle of a ride. Several companies make them—think of them as a "spare tire" for your horse. You'll need to follow the manufacturer's instructions to ensure you buy a boot that fits your horse properly. Should she lose a shoe on trail, put the hoof boot on, then head back to the barn, and call the farrier for an appointment.

Halter and lead rope: If your horse isn't wearing a combination halter/bridle, always bring a halter and lead rope. Many people have their horses wear the halter and lead rope, running the lead rope loosely along one side of the horse's neck and looping it over the horn. Just make sure you do not tie the lead rope around the horn, as it could get caught on a passing branch or object. Remember that you can never tie your horse with her bridle, so a halter and lead rope can come in handy.

Pocket knife: This can be useful for a number of applications. Cutting your horse free if she accidentally gets caught or tangled on something, or making a makeshift notch or hole in your tack in an emergency are two examples.

Hoof pick: Bring one in case something gets lodged in your horse's hoof. Foldable hoof picks are small and easy to pack.

Compass or GPS and map: If you're riding in an unfamiliar area or you plan to blaze some new trails, pack a compass or a GPS, and know how to use it. State and national parks usually have trail maps, and when available, take a map of the area where you're riding.

Twine and duct tape: These can be handy for any number of uses, including broken tack.

Water bottle and collapsible bucket: Take a water bottle for yourself. If water faucets are available, also pack a collapsible bucket for your horse.

Food: Depending on how long you're going to be out, take along food. If it's a short ride, take a snack, such as an energy bar.

Sunscreen and insect repellent: Be sure to use these beforehand, but take them along as well in case you need to reapply them.

Additional items to consider: You may want to take water purification tables, a whistle, a flashlight, a survival blanket (small, space-age emergency blanket), and an EpiPen if you're allergic to insect stings. If you need to tie your horse to a tree, pack a tree saver, which protects the tree from rope rubs.

How to Pack

Of course, daylong rides require additional supplies, such as meals and extra water. These items are easily accommodated in large saddlebags, and insulated bags can help keep items cool or hot. If you pack food, don't get carried away with heavy items, such as ice packs. Instead, freeze a bottle of water, which you can drink after lunch. Avoid heavy or bulky food containers; pick snacks and sandwiches that won't get ruined if they're a bit crushed during travel. Pack lunch and snacks in baggies or cling wrap, and always dispose of trash in a bin or take it home with you.

Pack your saddlebags so that there's an even amount of weight on each side, and take into consideration your weight, the weight of your tack, and the weight of your saddlebags and gear when deciding if a load is too much for your horse. How much is too much varies greatly. It depends on your horse's size, health, and build. An experienced trainer or veterinarian familiar with you and your horse can help you assess an acceptable weight load.

In addition to packing carefully, always tell someone where you plan to ride and how long you'll be gone. This holds true whether you're riding alone or with others. Even if you don't know exactly how long you'll be out, at least give the latest time possible; for example, "We'll be back by sunset for sure." This way, if something does occur on trail and you're unable to make it back to the stable without assistance, someone will know where you were riding and can send help.

Health and Safety Considerations
There are a number of potential safety hazards on trail. Although rare, attacks by people and animals happen. Stinging insects and poisonous plants and snakes are dangers, as is bad weather. You must take proper precautions for riding in both hot and cold temperatures. It's important to be able to recognize signs of stress in your horse and know what to do.

Natural Hazards
When trail riding, you must prepare for natural hazards, including plants and wildlife. Learn what poisonous plants are in your area, and watch for them on trail. Then make sure your horse doesn't grab a mouthful, and don't tie her or let her graze near these plants. To be completely safe, don't let your horse graze on trail. If you do and your horse isn't used to eating fresh grass, don't let her graze for more than a half hour.

Learn about what, if any, poisonous snakes populate the areas where you ride. Splint boots or sport boots can help protect a horse's legs from bearing the full brunt of a snake bite; also ask your veterinarian about any other protective measures you can take should your horse be bitten. For the most part, snakes are shy, so staying on the lookout for them and giving them a wide berth can be the best preventive measure.

Bees, wasps, and hornets are more likely attackers, especially if you accidentally disrupt a nest or hive in the ground or in a tree. If one or two land on you or your horse, try to quietly flick them away without killing them or making a big scene, which could attract additional hive members. Stay calm and walk slowly out of the area. However, if you disrupt an entire nest or hive and have a whole swarm bent on attacking you, exit the area quickly, running if it's safe to do so. When you've left their territory, try to carefully remove any stingers left by bees. If your horse has many stings, she may break out in hives. If she's been stung multiple times, call the veterinarian and head slowly back to the barn. If you're allergic, carry an EpiPen with you whenever and wherever you ride.

Human and Animal Threats

If you're riding alone, trust your instincts, and don't think you're immune from danger because you're on a horse. For a human assailant to attack on trail, he or she will need to get close to your horse, so remember that it's OK to tell someone they can't pet your horse or to move away quickly if you're feeling threatened. If someone grabs you or your reins, turn your horse in a circle away from your attacker so your horse's hind end moves toward the perpetrator; then trot, canter, or gallop away.

Dogs often bark at horses and frighten them. If you encounter a dog off leash and the owner is nearby, ask the owner to hold the dog or put her on a leash. Even if the dog isn't going to bite, your horse may kick the dog if she runs behind the horse or under her legs. When no owners are in sight and a dog is approaching you aggressively, don't try to run. In most cases, this will just incite the dog to chase your horse. Yelling at the dog in an angry, loud voice and telling her to go home often will do the trick. Turning your horse to face the dog and taking a step or two toward her also may be effective—this shows her you're not prey and are much larger. If you ride an area where you repeatedly run into loose, aggressive dogs, report them to local authorities.

If you like to ride with your own dog, make sure she's under voice control and that where you plan to ride allows off-leash dogs. Ensure your horse is used to the dog running about nearby while you ride. Riding along streets or across private property with a loose dog is never a good idea.

If you ride in bear country, check park reports on local bear activity, and consider canceling your ride if bears have been active in the area. Any time you ride in bear country, consider attaching a trail bell to your horse's breast collar. In addition, try to talk or otherwise make noise as you ride down trails, and, whenever possible, ride in a group. By making noise as you head down the trail, you'll avoid surprising a bear. If you see a bear cub, leave the area, as mama is not far off. If you encounter an adult bear, don't make direct eye contact or approach the bear. Instead, stay calm, and try to slowly exit the area. Do not appear threatening, or you may aggravate the bear. Grizzlies and black bears have somewhat different behaviors, so familiarize yourself with the habits of the bears in your area. You can carry bear spray as an emergency defense, but keep it handy and remember that it's effective only at close range. When camping in bear country, follow all park guidelines for food storage so as not to attract bears to your campsite.

Mountain lions are another large predator that may share your trails, especially in the West. However, mountain lions are not known to attack horseback riders. If you do come face to face with a mountain lion, look big. Yell at him, move your arms, and if he tries to approach, throw things (if available) at him. Don't run, as

These Rocky Mountain Horses have no problem being accompanied by a friendly, well-trained dog on a ride through Fenelon Falls, Ontario.

this may incite him to chase you. Your superior size when mounted paired with your seeming lack of fear could send him on his way!

Trail Conditions

If you ride at night, stay away from traffic, and ride only on trails you're familiar with. Night riding is not the time to explore unfamiliar terrain, as your horse is more likely to stumble, and you're more likely to get lost. If you take a flashlight or glow sticks, get your horse used to these things at night at home before you hit the trail. If you'll be riding anywhere near cars or other vehicles, wear reflective gear.

Footing can be another natural hazard, day or night. Any time the footing seems slippery or otherwise dangerous, consider dismounting and leading your horse. Watch out for hard or extremely deep footing, and don't travel faster than a walk through these areas to avoid stressing your horse's legs or hooves.

Whenever you ride, always check the weather forecast. There are online weather sites where you can see the hour-by-hour outlook. If there are flash flood warnings or thunder and lightning are predicted, don't ride.

Many people enjoy riding in the snow; however, avoid ice. Keep in mind that ice forms quickest and lingers longest in the shade and on bridges. Remember, too, that deep snow is hard for your horse to walk through. Choose your footing and trails carefully, and stick to terrain you're familiar with. Make sure your horse has adequate traction (see Preventive Maintenance), keep the ride within her fitness level, and remember that it may take a good deal of time to cool her out and dry her off afterward. For this reason, some people choose to body clip or partially body clip their horses for cold weather riding. If you choose to clip, you will have to provide your horse adequate blankets and shelter to replace her natural protection.

During a heat spell, avoid riding in the middle of the day. Early morning and evenings are usually cooler. You may need to slow your pace and take shorter rides. Especially avoid high heat combined with high humidity. To determine if it's too hot to ride, add the outside temperature to the relative humidity. If the number is under 130, it's usually OK to ride. However, heavily muscled or overweight horses will have a harder time staying cool.

Heat Exhaustion and Dehydration

Hot weather can cause heat exhaustion or heatstroke and dehydration in horses, just as it does in people, especially when paired

An owner pinches the skin of his horse to check the animal's condition; if the skin stays pinched for a moment, the horse is dehydrated.

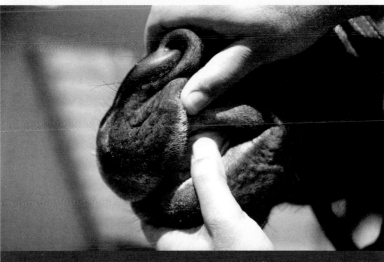

In another dehydration test, the owner briefly presses a thumb into the gums to see how quickly color returns when the pressure is released.

On a hot Texas day, a man hoses down his Quarter Horse to both cool the animal off and remove sweat, which is drying to the skin.

with hard work and inadequate water. If you suspect your horse is becoming dehydrated, pinch the skin on her neck. It should immediately return to its normal position. If the skin you pinched stays "tented" for a moment or very slowly goes back to normal, your horse is becoming or is already dehydrated. Another test is pulling up her upper lip and pressing the gums above her top front teeth with your thumb. This will push the pink pigment out. The color should return to normal within two seconds. If not, this is another indicator she's dehydrated. Stop working her, and offer her water.

Move an overheated horse to the shade. Contrary to old wives' tales, cold water applied to a hot horse is actually a good thing. Hose or bucket off your horse, pushing the water away with a sweat scraper so fresh, cold water is constantly being applied to her skin. Signs of actual heatstroke include a body temperature above 105 degrees Fahrenheit, rapid breathing and pulse, weakness or depression, and refusal to eat or work. In severe cases of heatstroke, horses can collapse or go into convulsions. If you suspect your horse is suffering from heat exhaustion, heatstroke, or dehydration, call your veterinarian.

A horse that's not overheated or dehydrated but just generally tired from the day's work should also be rested. When a horse is genuinely worn out and pushed beyond her fitness level, she will be more likely to stumble or injure herself and will be at risk for a number of health problems. Signs of a tired horse may include stopping, stumbling, slowing down, lowering the head, sweating, or heavy breathing. Head back to the barn slowly, stopping to rest as needed.

Just as you pack your water bottle for a trail ride, you'll need to consider your horse's water needs. If you're going out for only a couple of hours, water is not a huge concern, but you must plan ahead on longer rides.

Streams

You'll want to teach your horse to drink from streams and other bodies of water, but not all horses will do so readily. In fact, some horses don't like to drink unfamiliar water at all. The best way to encourage your horse to drink from streams is to ride with another horse that's comfortable crossing water and drinking from natural water sources. Every time you reach a natural water source, let the horse stop by the water's edge and rest. Place your horse close enough to her friend so that she feels relaxed, but not so close that either feels crowded. Let her smell the water, put her foot in if she wants, and watch her friend. With enough repetition, if your horse is thirsty, she'll most likely give natural water sources a try.

Collapsible Water Buckets

If natural water sources are not available or your horse refuses to drink from them, you can carry a collapsible water bucket for your horse. These are available from several manufacturers and are light and easily packable. Rinse it out thoroughly with your home water

A rider pauses on the trail to allow his horse to drink from a clear stream. Stop for a drink at all water crossings.

to get any "new" or chemical smells out. Introduce your horse to the bucket at home. You may even want to fill it with water and set or attach it near her normal water bucket so she's familiar with it and associates it with drinking. Then, when you're on trail, you can fill it at any available water sources. State and national parks often have water fountains or spigots you can use.

If you ride on designated horse trails, there may be water troughs on trail or at trailheads. It's best to use your collapsible water bucket by filling it from the spigot rather than letting your horse drink out of the communal trough—you don't want your horse catching a virus that was passed along from another horse that recently drank there.

Whatever the water source—streams, fountains, or spigots—offer your horse water at every opportunity. She'll need more water on hot days, just as you do.

Lame, Tying Up, Colic

If you're out on trail and your horse begins to limp, tie up, colic, or otherwise act unwell, follow these steps to evaluate the situation:

Lame: First, check her feet to make sure there is nothing lodged in a hoof. If she's non-weight-bearing lame, call for help; otherwise, hand walk her back to the stable, and call your veterinarian for a consultation.

Tying up: A horse that is tying up may demonstrate muscle stiffness, including a short stride, an elevated pulse or respiration (or both), sweating, and other signs of severe discomfort. If your horse is tying up, you'll need to call for help, as this horse should not be forced to walk. Your veterinarian will help you treat a current episode of tying up and offer diet and exercise tips to prevent future attacks.

Colic: Colic is a general term that means there's pain somewhere in your horse's abdomen. A colicky horse will often bite or kick at her stomach, stretch her front and hind legs out, or try to roll. Dismount and begin walking your horse toward the stable. If her condition doesn't rapidly improve, call your veterinarian en route so he or she can meet you at the stable as soon as possible.

Checking Vital Signs

Anytime your horse is lame or you notice a change in demeanor, it is wise to check her vital signs, including heart rate, respiration, and temperature. Every horse owner should learn how to take a horse's vitals and memorize the averages for each. Your first aid kit should have a horse rectal thermometer for taking your horse's temperature wherever you go. However, keep in mind that your horse's vitals are affected by exercise. Her heart rate, respiration, and temperature will rise when she exerts herself. Practice taking her vitals while you're out on trail so you know what is "normal" in different weather conditions and at different exertion levels. You can keep a reference sheet in your first aid kit. If your horse is not acting quite right on trail and her vitals are out of range, something could be wrong. Here are instructions on how to check your horse's vitals:

Heart rate or pulse: A horse's average resting pulse rate is 30 to 42 beats per minute. Take the horse's pulse manually in several different locations: the left underside of her lower jaw, the inside back of her knee, or at the artery just below her fetlock. These large arteries may take a moment to locate. Once you find one, press your index and middle fingers gently against it until you can feel your horse's pulse, then count how many beats you feel during a 15-second period. Multiply that number by four. You also may listen with a stethoscope behind your horse's left elbow in front of where your girth or cinch would go; you also may be able to feel it. Count each lub-dub of the heart as one beat. Again, time yourself for 15 seconds, then multiply the number of beats you counted by four.

Respiration: A horse's average respiratory rate is 12 to 20 breaths per minute. To check your horse's respiration, watch her nostrils or put your hand in front of one to feel the air coming out. You also can watch her flank. Count each inhale and exhale as one breath. If you have a stethoscope, listen after placing it on your horse's windpipe.

Temperature: A horse's average temperature is 99.5 to 101.5 degrees Fahrenheit. To take your horse's temperature, you'll need a traditional horse thermometer with the mercury shaken down or a digital horse thermometer. Either should have a string and clip attached so the thermometer can't get lost inside or outside the horse! A horse's temperature is taken rectally, so lubricate the end of the thermometer with petroleum or K-Y jelly, or even sali-

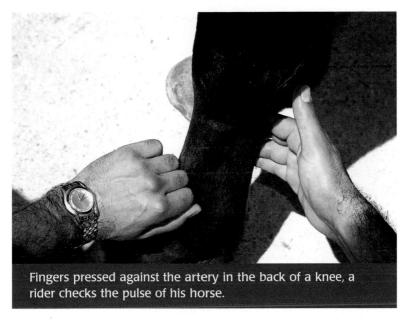

Fingers pressed against the artery in the back of a knee, a rider checks the pulse of his horse.

va in a pinch. Read the thermometer's instructions as to how far to put it in and how long to leave it in. Traditional thermometers usually must be left in for three minutes, and digital ones often can be read in one minute.

If you'd prefer to have someone show you how to take your horse's vitals, ask your veterinarian. Most will be happy to do so and offer suggestions on when you should call them. However, anytime your horse's vitals are out of the normal range, it's a good idea to call the veterinarian for further instructions.

For extreme emergencies, it's helpful to have programmed into your cell phone a contact person who has a truck and a trailer. If a road is accessible near the trail you're on, it may be advisable to trailer your horse home or to the veterinary hospital.

Cooling Out

Always walk your horse when headed back to the barn. This accomplishes two things. One, it shows your horse she may not rush home.

On a trail in Oro, Ontario, horse and rider proceed at a leisurely pace. Always walk on the way home.

Horses naturally speed up on the way home because they know they'll be fed, rested, and safe there. Don't make this habit worse by jogging or loping toward home. Two, walking home cools your horse out. It allows her heart rate and temperature to begin to return to normal. If your horse is still sweating or breathing heavily when you get back to the barn, dismount, loosen her cinch, and hand walk her until she's back to normal. If your horse is wet from rain, towel her off. When it's cold outside, you'll want to cover your horse with a cooler until she dries off.

If it's a warm day, you can hose your horse down after a ride, starting at her legs to let her get used to the water temperature before running it over her sensitive back; or you can get a bucket of water and sponge her sweaty areas. In cold weather, if you don't have access to hot water, towel your horse off, put the cooler on until she's dry, then brush her. It's important to remove the sweat because sweat contains salt, which will dry out your horse's coat and make her itchy. Always check your horse's feet before you put her away to make sure she didn't pick up any rocks or debris on trail.

While preparation and safety considerations can seem overwhelming, with a little thought and practice, you'll be in a routine in no time, and you and your horse will both be better off for it.

In Good Company

Most trail riders enjoy the camaraderie of riding with a friend or two, and if you trail ride often, you may eventually find yourself going out with a larger group or participating in an organized group ride. When no friends are available, you may choose to go out on the trail alone. Each of these situations presents unique challenges and opportunities for you and your horse.

Riding with Experienced Friends

If you or your horse are new to trail riding or you're heading into uncharted territory, such as near roads or through water crossings, riding with an experienced horse and rider team is invaluable. As herd animals, horses look to their peers for safety. When their friends are nervous, it puts them on alert; when their friends are calm, it helps assure them that everything's OK. That doesn't mean a nervous horse will be 100 percent calm around a relaxed horse, but the levelheaded buddy will certainly have a beneficial effect on an excited horse.

In addition to providing a calming influence, the experienced horse and rider team can lead the way over water crossings and past traffic and screaming kids. The veteran horse can show the novice mount that it's no big deal, and the more experienced rider can offer tips and advice to the novice.

The experienced team can also help you work on your leadership skills if your horse doesn't like to be in the lead and feels more comfortable following. Wait for a quiet place on the trail, then ask your friend to let you take a turn in the lead as a learning opportunity for your horse. If your horse is slow or tries to turn around, encourage him forward with gentle leg pressure and light hands. Speak to him encouragingly, and praise him with a stroke or scratch. At first, the two of you may lead for only a short time. Continue taking turns with the other rider. You want your horse to be as comfortable leading as he is following. If you always follow, eventually he may tolerate only being behind another horse. Then, what will happen when you go out with a less experienced team that wants you to lead or when you go riding alone?

Riding Etiquette with Others

Having good trail etiquette is about more than just having nice manners; it's also about safety. Following the guidelines below will make for a more pleasurable trail ride for everyone involved and will prevent many unnecessary accidents. In addition, it will teach your horse the proper way to behave in a group of horses and riders, which will become all the more important when you ride with unfamiliar or unpredictable horses.

Following Manners

When you and your horse are riding with others, maintain one horse length between horses. Some horses crowd the horse in front of them—they feel comfortable only if their heads are practically buried in their friend's tail. However nice and accommodating the lead horse is, this is not acceptable. Someday you'll want to ride with others, and many horses will kick when followed this closely. It also puts you in danger should the lead horse turn, spook, or back unexpectedly. Teach your horse to maintain one horse-length distance from the lead horse.

If he frets and fidgets at this distance, focus his attention on you by asking him to give his shoulder. For example, apply pressure at the girth with your left leg while tipping his nose

A Morgan mare and her rider lead another trail riding pair through a stream in New York's Otter Creek.

Two riders and their mounts walk companionably through a field. Although some horses prefer being leaders and others followers, all horses should practice both roles.

slightly to the left and maintaining light contact on your right rein to keep him from turning in a circle. This should shift his shoulders to the right. Try it in the other direction as well. When he's concentrating on what you're asking and where his feet are, he'll be less likely to fret over the distance between himself and his friend. This can also be a good time to practice changing positions. Play leapfrog, with each horse and rider spending a minute or two in the lead position, and then practice following a horse length behind. Your experienced friend and veteran lead horse will once again come in handy as a good example and a patient teacher.

Never trot, canter, or gallop up to the horse in front of you. This can frighten the horse in front and cause an accident. Instead, call out to the rider in front of you, and ask him or her to slow down or stop and wait for you.

Leading Manners

When you're in the lead, it's important to keep an eye on those behind you. If the person behind you falls back more than two horse lengths or is having trouble with his or her horse, stop and wait for the rider to catch up or for the horse to calm down. It's rude to charge on ahead, as horses often get antsy when separated. Sometimes the rider behind can't get the horse to walk fast enough. A rider in this situation may pull back to keep the horse from running, and in the end the horse may jig, a combination of a walk and jog that's slow and bouncy, going slower than ever. If this happens, stop your horse and wait until they are a horse length behind you. Then it may be time to leapfrog, changing positions until the horse has refocused and calmed down.

Often, one horse walks significantly faster than another. If this is the case, the rider on the slow horse can encourage him to walk faster by gently squeezing his sides and releasing the pressure when he walks faster, even if the improvement is slight. The rider on the faster horse can encourage him to slow down a bit by sitting deeply in the saddle and perhaps taking up gentle contact with his mouth, releasing the pressure anytime he slows his walk (remember that even minor improvements must be rewarded by a release in pressure). But in the end, the faster horse may have to stop frequently and wait for his friend, or if he's following, stop briefly to maintain his safe following distance of one horse length.

The lead rider is responsible for informing the rider or riders behind if there is an obstacle or something else to avoid in the trail. For example, calling out "Hole on the left" can warn riders that there's a dangerous hole on the left side of the trail. An arm signal that your group decides on ahead of time can signal riders behind you to stop if you're riding in a group too large for riders several horses back to hear.

All riders should be in agreement before picking up the pace to a trot or faster. Simply taking off at a faster speed can cause the horses behind you to bolt.

Riding in a Group

Before going out with a group of riders, find out what kind of terrain they plan to cover. Are there water crossings? Will you have to ride on or near a road? Is your horse prepared for these situations? Is it a steep ride? Find out how long the ride will be. If your horse isn't in shape for hills or long rides, pass until he is. Also inquire about what speed they plan to ride. They may like to trot or canter where you normally walk; this is an indication they're not the group for you. If you don't already know their horses, ask if they're experienced or calm. Horses that tend to get nervous will only be worse around other nervous horses. If you're going on an organized trail ride with a large group of riders, expect some of the horses to misbehave, and don't sign up until you're sure your horse is ready for the terrain, the length, and the experience in general. Riding in a group of three or more horses can be exciting and nerve-racking for

The following rider and horse appear to be maintaining a good distance from the leading team on a trail in Texas. Always maintain one horse length between horses.

your horse if he's not used to it. There is a lot going on, probably horses he's never met, and many things for him to take in. If possible, increase the size of group you ride in slowly, perhaps riding with one person first, then two, then three or four, and so on. When you ride in a large group for the first time, such as on an organized trail ride, go with an experienced horse your horse already knows and has bonded with. That way the two of you can stick together—a safe harbor for your horse amid the chaos.

Horses with the fastest walking speed tend to head toward the front on large rides, with slower horses falling toward the back. Feel free to hang back or move forward (safely and without crowding other riders) until you find a group you're comfortable in. If you get behind a nervous horse or a rider that lets her horse bolt forward whenever they fall behind, reposition yourself close to a more consistent pair. Always practice etiquette when passing others. Most people pass on the left side. Whenever you go to pass another horse or hiker or biker, call out "Passing on the left" so the person doesn't accidentally get in your way.

A slower rider lags behind the group during a trail ride. It's important to make sure no one gets left behind the group.

You'll usually be able to find many friendly riders willing to offer advice or help you if you run into trouble on a large group ride. However, don't accept suggestions, help, or advice you're not comfortable with. You should have prepared ahead of time for whatever terrain or obstacles you may encounter on a group ride, but horses aren't always predictable. For example, although your horse may be crossing water consistently at home, the new setting may cause him trouble. If you reach a water crossing or other obstacle that your horse doesn't want to cross, you may have people offering to pull him across or force him. Stick to your normal training philosophy. Take your time, and don't let others pressure you. Move to the back of the line so your horse can see the other horses navigate the obstacle, and you won't be holding everyone else up. This is another time that an experienced friend can come in handy. With someone by your side, you don't have to worry about "being left."

In addition, you may have all the trail manners in the world, but not everyone does. If a horse is crowding you from behind, ask the person to give your horse a little more space. Tying a red ribbon in your horse's tail indicates he kicks and will also encourage others to give you a bit more space if your horse gets antsy when crowded. If your horse is a kicker, keep a careful eye on him. Before a horse kicks, he will usually pin back his ears or swish his tail. If you recognize the signs, turn him immediately to face the horse behind him. This will prevent him from kicking by moving his hind end away from the other horse and diffusing the situation.

In groups of six or fewer, ask if riders are willing to take turns in different positions, just as you may when riding with a friend. Taking turns in different positions is good practice for all the horses.

Water crossings are another place to watch your manners. It's important that everyone stay nearby while each horse gets a turn to drink. Letting your horse drink and then heading down the trail will make the horses behind you nervous about being left and discourage them from taking a good, long drink.

It's important for someone on a group ride to assume leadership and make sure no one gets left behind or feels uncomfortable. On large group rides, it's advisable to assign a lead rider and a sweep rider, who brings up the rear and keeps the group together. Don't be afraid to speak up if you need the other riders to wait, if you see another rider falling behind, or if people are not maintaining safe following distances. Being conscientious can prevent accidents.

Riding Alone

Unless your horse is already accustomed to riding alone, he'll most likely be frightened by the prospect. Remember that horses are herd animals—safety in numbers is part of their genetics and natural survival instincts. When asked to ride out on trail alone, most horses won't want to leave the barn, and once they do, they'll be nervous and on the lookout, knowing there are no herd members to alert them to danger. For this reason, you'll need to be a strong leader and rider if you take your horse out alone. You also must be patient while getting your horse accustomed to riding by himself.

If your horse is not comfortable going out on trail alone, start the training process by taking "barn walks" around your stable area. If you have access to an arena, round pen, or pasture with safe footing, work your horse first. Ask him to walk, jog, lope, circle, back up, and side-pass. When your workout is over and your horse seems a bit tired, take your barn walk and eventually a short trail ride as you cool down. Making the trail ride a relaxing reward will help your horse think of it as a welcome break from the arena and hard work.

Once he's comfortable barn cruising, head down the street or trail a short distance. When your horse gets nervous or tries to turn around and go home, put him to work. Ask him to give his shoulder by tipping his nose to one side with your right rein and leg or left rein and leg, or ask him to ride in zigzags or perform several small circles or side-passes in each direction. When his attention is focused back on you, ask him to walk a few more yards down the trail. If he does so willingly and calmly, pat him and head home. If he continues to be nervous, try to focus his attention and calm him down with your exercises. Ideally, you want heading home to be your idea, but just as with desensitization work, you don't want to push him too far out of his comfort zone either.

Another option, also detailed in chapter 7, is to go out ahead of time and leave a bucket with a bit of grain at the point where your horse usually starts to get antsy heading away from home. Stop and let him eat the grain, and then continue a bit farther before heading home. You can continue to move the bucket farther away and eventually do away with it altogether once your horse understands leaving home can be rewarding.

Your horse may hurry on the way home. If he does, try your exercises again. You'll find which ones work to refocus his attention on you—whether it's giving his shoulder or side-passing—and use them as needed to show your horse that acting up means more work for him. The idea is to get your horse to listen to you and teach him

A rider and Paint Horse walk around the stable area. If your horse isn't used to trail riding alone, start by taking barn walks.

A solitary horse and rider travel down a trail. Most levelheaded horses can become comfortable riding alone.

that it's easier to behave; he'll be rewarded with a release of pressure from your hands and legs.

You can also use food as a training tool on the way home by stopping to let your horse graze for a few moments when he rushes. Pat him and show him there's no hurry.

Continue this routine of ring work then short rides for as long as it takes. Over several days, weeks, or months, your horse will be traveling farther and farther from home without acting up. He may always be more nervous alone than with others, but the important thing is that he listens to you, responds to your requests, and accepts you as his leader, even when he's nervous.

Following safety precautions is even more important when you're riding alone. Remember to tell someone where you'll be going and how long you'll be gone, and always carry a charged cell phone.

Practicing good manners when riding in groups and patience with your horse when riding alone will pay off in the long run with safer, more enjoyable trail rides.

Behavior Problems

All trail horses act up in one way or another and for one reason or another. However, not all behavior problems are created equal. Some have hidden causes that take detective work to uncover; others are only minor annoyances. The worst behavior problems are downright dangerous and must be properly addressed to avoid injury. Read on to learn about common causes for acting out and solutions for the major bad habits trail riders face.

Why Horses Act Up

Before trying to "fix" your horse's behavior problem, investigate why she's acting up. Horses don't misbehave just to make you mad or to scare you. There's usually a reason.

Below are a few possible causes for behavior problems, and a horse may be influenced by more than one of these at any given time.

Pain: Because horses can't tell us when and where they hurt, they often show they're in pain through behavior. For example, if your horse flinches when you curry one shoulder but not the other, she's probably telling you her shoulder hurts. If she hollows her back when you curry it or when you place the saddle on her, this probably indicates back pain. Limping, of course, signifies a problem in her hoof, leg, hip, or shoulder.

Other problems can be more subtle. Ulcers, for example, can manifest in a horse that's less willing to work or is generally grumpier. If your horse's behavior suddenly or inexplicably changes, pain may be the cause.

Severe or chronic problems will require a veterinarian's visit right away, but utilize your routine appointments—for shots, teeth floating, and such—to ask your veterinarian about your concerns. Even if you think it's a stupid question, ask. It's better to investigate any suspicions.

Ill-fitting equipment: Surprisingly, poor saddle fit can cause a whole host of behavior problems, from bucking, bolting, and rearing to apprehension about moving out or going forward. A poor-fitting or incorrectly adjusted bit can cause a horse to avoid pressure from the bit, either by raising her head too high, lowering it too much, or tossing it. See chapter 2 for more information on choosing the right tack and adjusting it correctly.

Inadequate training: A horse without a solid foundation of basic training will not understand how to respond to the rider's aids—hands, legs, seat, weight, and voice. This horse may toss her head or put her head up when you apply pressure to the bit rather than lowering her head and giving to the bit, as most horses are trained to do. She may misinterpret or ignore your aids, running through or around them. If you suspect this is the problem, you'll need to find a reputable trainer or instructor who can work with your horse or, preferably, you and your horse. (Chapter 1 offers guidelines for finding the right instructor.)

Rider error: Just as the untrained horse can misinterpret aids, the inexperienced rider can give faulty aids. For example, if you don't have a lot of riding experience, you'll probably bounce at the jog or trot and lope or canter. Your legs may jiggle against the horse's sides unintentionally, or your hands may wiggle around, pulling the reins. In addition, you may not know how to use your weight or seat correctly, or you may pull your reins out too far, up too high, or too sharply. These mixed signals can irritate a horse, cause her to go too fast or too slow, or make her "dead" in the mouth and sides, meaning she ignores the rider's constant jabbing and pulling. If you can't deliver clear, consistent, purposeful cues to your horse, sign up for

A rider tries to deal with a mount that is acting up. If your horse has problems regularly, investigate possible causes to find a long-term solution.

riding lessons in an arena. No one is born knowing how to ride, and even natural riders need practice and guidance.

Bad habits: Many bad habits are a result of rider error. You may have purchased a horse that has an ingrained bad habit or she may have developed one with you because one of you wasn't trained or confident enough to stop the horse from grabbing grass along the trail or from running home. Soon, the horse has decided these things are part of trail riding. Bad habits, as we all know, can be hard to break. You can retrain her, but it will take patience and a certain level of skill. If your horse's behavior is beyond your capabilities, you'll need to hire a trainer to work with her or a riding instructor who can work with you and your horse. See chapter 1 for tips on choosing a trainer or riding instructor.

Insecurity or lack of trust: To follow your cues willingly, your horse must respect you as the herd leader and trust your judgment. A horse that thinks she's in charge or believes you may lead her into unsafe situations will often disobey. The best way to establish yourself as a herd leader and gain your horse's trust is to be a confident, consistent leader. Always cue your horse with the same clear aids, and don't let her get away with certain behavior one day and not another. Keep your emotions in check, and never lead your horse into an unsafe situation or one beyond her capabilities or yours. Remember that anytime you work with your horse, you're working on your relationship. If you let your horse crowd you on the lead line or in her corral, you're teaching her she's the leader. Use every opportunity—from grooming to riding—to reinforce your leadership role.

Wrong horse: Of course, even the most confident and capable rider can't make an extremely high-strung horse a relaxed and trustworthy trail partner. Certain horses just don't have the temperaments to make safe or enjoyable trail mounts. Refer to chapter 1 for more information on evaluating a trail horse *before* you buy her.

Excess energy: Even the best of horses can act up if they have been locked up without exercise or stimulation for days on end. A frisky horse may buck, bolt, jig, or spook more easily than normal. Remember that your trail horse is an athlete. She's being asked to carry a rider over varied terrain, including hard surfaces and hills. Don't leave your horse locked in a stall or corral for days and then expect her to perform calmly and without injury to herself or you! Make sure she gets exercised several times a week. If she lives in a small pen or stall, try to turn her out in a paddock or pasture daily for some free time. Horses are social creatures, so turn her out with or near friends. Having other horses in adjoining pens will usually make for a happier horse.

Diet: You have no doubt heard the saying "you are what you eat," and to a certain extent that's true. A horse that's not getting the nutrition she needs may be stubborn or lazy, and a pleasure horse on a high-energy diet may have excess energy, causing her to buck, bolt, or shy. An average trail horse without health problems will likely get all the nutrition and calories she needs from high-quality forage, including hay and grass. Grain is often unnecessary. Have your hay or pasture professionally analyzed by a lab to tell you exactly what nutrients may be lacking, then work with your veterinarian to come up with the optimal diet for your horse's needs.

Weather: Even the weather can affect a horse's behavior. Windy days are notorious for causing horses to be extra frisky or spooky because wind causes tree branches and debris to blow about.

There are a number of reasons horses act up. Don't assume your horse is just being naughty or that it's purely a training issue. Investigate each of these possibilities to determine the best course of action to correct any behavior problem, and remember that more than one of the issues listed above may be influencing your horse's actions.

Being Proactive

Once you get to know your horse, it's often possible to tell when she's "about to blow." You will begin to spot the body language that indicates she's going to spook, buck, or bolt. Her neck may stiffen as her head pops up and her ears dart forward. Perhaps she resists your leg, and her entire body becomes straight as board. Every horse is different, so learn to recognize your horse's individual signs of trouble. If you can do this, you can ride proactively to prevent a bad behavior.

The minute you notice your horse's warning signs, focus her attention on you to diffuse the situation. There are several ways to do this. You can try asking your horse to bend in a tight circle or to move her shoulder over toward one direction or the other, or to bend her head around in one direction and come to a stop. What works for one horse may not work for another, so experiment until you find the best preventive action.

Remember that how you feel will influence your horse's behavior. If you're tense or afraid, your horse will pick up on this. Breathe deeply when your horse gets upset, sit up tall, and decide on a course

This experienced equestrian pulls her horse into a tight circle to head off undesirable behavior.

of action so you can act confidently and purposefully as the leader. If you do not feel confident handling your horse's behavior, or if the bad behavior has become chronic, seek help from an experienced trainer or riding instructor. (See chapter 1 for suggestions on finding a good trainer.)

Any of the problem behaviors described below can cause a fall. If you fall, always assess your health first. Call for help from fellow riders or on your cell phone if you're injured. Deal with catching your horse next. The first rule is never to chase a horse on foot or on horseback. Approach the horse slowly. Carry a handful of grass or other treat if it's available, and speak sweetly to your horse. If you have friends with you, your horse most likely won't stray far from the other horses. However, if she eludes you and bolts for home, begin retracing your steps. There is a good chance you can find her safe along the way. Once she's caught, never punish her, or she'll be all the harder to catch next time.

Annoying Problems

Although any misbehavior can have more serious consequences, the following behaviors could be classified as annoying rather than dangerous. Still, they're enough to ruin a good ride and may indicate larger problems, so investigate possible causes thoroughly, and then take a patient and systematic approach to addressing your horse's behavior. Remember that horses, like children, will respond best to consistency. If you allow your horse to grab grass some days and not others, for example, she will not learn that grass grabbing is against the rules. As discussed above (this cannot be overemphasized), if you're not making headway in your retraining program, seek help from an experienced trainer or riding instructor.

The Barn-Sour Horse

Barn-sour horses either don't want to leave home or they want to head home too quickly. If you're trying to ride alone, this may be an

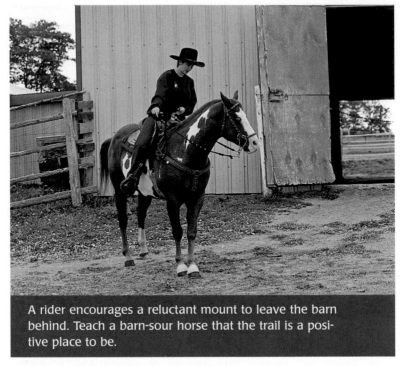

A rider encourages a reluctant mount to leave the barn behind. Teach a barn-sour horse that the trail is a positive place to be.

exhibition of herd-bound behavior—your horse simply doesn't want to leave her friends.

A horse that doesn't want to leave the barn may need to learn it is more work to resist than to comply. For example, as you leave the barn and your horse stops or tries to turn around, put her to work. Ask her to perform several tight turns, first in one direction and then in another. Or ask her to do a turn on the haunches, where her hind end stays still and her front legs cross over each other and move to the left or right. A turn on the forehand is another maneuver: in this one, the front end stays relatively still, and the hind legs move around. Any request you can make that focuses your horse's attention on you and makes her apply herself may help. Then ask her to move forward again. If she complies, pat and praise her. Put her back to work whenever she resists. (See chapter 6 for more tips.)

The same theory applies to horses that hurry home: make them work. Every time your horse starts to speed up when you didn't request it, sit deeply in the saddle, apply gentle pressure to the reins, and ask her to slow down to the speed you had previously requested. If she doesn't comply or continues to speed up, put her to work with turns and maneuvers. It will probably take a great deal of

If your horse refuses to go far from home or tries to hurry back, have her perform a focused exercise such as this turn on the haunches.

Rider and horse go through a rigorous arena workout. A good workout beforehand can make a short trail ride seem a welcome relief.

patience and many training sessions before your horse realizes that resistance gets her nowhere. But if you are consistent with your approach, she'll eventually catch on.

Another tactic to help reverse your horse's thinking is to make the stable area a place of work and the trail ride a relaxing reward. If your horse doesn't like to leave the barn, work her in an arena or a paddock area with good footing. Make her walk, jog or trot, lope or canter, do circles, do side-passes, back up, and turn on haunches and forehand. Give her a good workout for her fitness level, then take her on a short, relaxing trail ride. Repeat this for several weeks, and your horse will most likely begin to relish her more leisurely trail

A Quarter Horse enjoys a snack on the trail. Teach a barn-sour horse that the trail can be pleasant by placing a bucket of grain along the way.

rides. For a horse that likes to speed home, try the opposite regimen: give her a good workout in the ring or paddock as soon as you return from a trail ride. This way, she doesn't associate returning home with an instant reward of food and rest.

You can also try using food to teach your horse that the trail is a great place to be. You can carry treats, dismounting and feeding them to your horse on the way out from the barn, or you can leave a bucket of grain at the approximate place your horse begins to resist leaving home. Let her eat the grain, ride a bit farther, and then turn around and head back. Slowly, you can move the grain farther and farther from home; eventually you will be able to wean your horse from it. You can use food on the return trip as well, stopping to let your horse graze a bit on the way back to teach her to take her time and relax.

Grass Grabbing

Grass grabbing is a minor problem compared with most, but it can be annoying. To avoid this bad habit, be strict with your horse. As you're riding along, do not allow your horse to eat because soon she'll be eating left and right, constantly looking for something to grab and sometimes pulling you forward in her dives for grass. If you choose to let your horse graze when you stop for a break, make sure she understands that it's your idea. Don't let her begin to eat until you say so.

If your horse already has a grass-grabbing habit, you can cure it with consistency and patience. Keep a watchful eye on her, and every time she reaches for a mouthful, squeeze her with your legs and turn her head in the opposite direction of the food. Turning her head is often easier than pulling back with both hands, which can instigate a tug-of-war that she is likely to win. Asking your horse to trot out with a firm bump from your legs when she tries to grab a mouthful can also distract her and show her that trying to snack on the trail is more trouble than it's worth.

For a horse that's a true, hardened grass grabber, you may need to purchase antigrazing reins. This device runs from your saddle along the top of your horse's neck to her bridle and prevents her from lowering her head enough to graze. However, use this piece of equipment only as a last resort. It's better to let your horse have full use of her neck to balance on steep hills or over difficult terrain. If you do use an antigrazing strap, make sure it's adjusted properly and is not too tight.

Head Tossing

Horses often toss their heads to evade pressure. Head tossing generally indicates the horse either needs dental work from a veterinari-

Taking preemptive action, this rider turns her horse's head away from the temptation of munching on all too handy vegetation along the trail.

an, a more comfortable bit or headstall, gentler guidance from the rider, or some additional training. It is not a problem that can be solved on trail.

A bit or headstall that pinches or puts pressure in the wrong places can also cause a horse to toss her head to avoid the discomfort. If the horse suffers from dental or mouth problems, bits can irritate or exacerbate the problem. A rider who puts constant pressure on the reins; who holds the reins too high, too low, or too far out; or who jerks on the reins can also cause a horse to toss her head. In this case, riding lessons are an easy solution. In addition, a horse

A horse that constantly tosses her head, as this one is doing, is usually suffering from ill-fitting tack, health issues, or a lack of training.

without proper training, one that has never learned to give to bit pressure, may also toss her head.

Jigging

When horses are in a hurry to get home or nervous, they often "jig," which is a bumpy cross between a walk and a jog or trot. This usually happens when you're trying to hold the horse back because she wants to rush forward. With all her energy held in, she begins to bounce up and down in a funny gait that is neither ground covering nor comfortable. As with any behavior problem, there are many ways to approach jigging. Try the different methods to see which approach works best for your horse.

If you're riding with another horse, your horse may be jigging because she wants to get in front. This can be a good time to play leapfrog, letting your horse lead for a few yards, then switching places for a few yards. You don't want your horse to think she always gets to lead, but you also need to teach her to follow slowly and patiently.

For a horse that jigs because she's in a hurry to get back to the barn, periodically try stopping, dismounting, and letting your horse graze for a couple of minutes. As with the barn-sour horse, the idea is to teach her to relax and take her time heading home.

Putting the jigging horse to work is another option. Asking your horse to perform maneuvers will not only refocus her attention on you but also allow you to release your death grip on the reins without fear of her rushing down the trail. First, ask your jigging horse to give her shoulder or move her shoulder in one direction or the other as she moves down the trail. To do this, tip her head to one side by squeezing your fingers until you can see her eye on that side. The opposite rein will maintain only light contact to keep her from turning in a circle. Then squeeze with your calf at the girth on the same side your horse's head is tipped toward. Her shoulder should move a few inches toward the opposite side. Hold her in this position for several feet down the trail, and then release all pressure, maintaining only a very light contact on her mouth. If she starts to jig again, ask her to give her shoulder in the other direction. Continue this pattern as you head down the trail. You can also try asking her to give her hind end by applying your leg pressure a few inches behind the girth on the same side as your squeezing rein.

Another maneuver you can try is the serpentine, which requires your horse to travel down the trail snaking in an S-shape, first bending in a half circle to the left, and then in a half circle to the right. If you're riding alone, you can try turning and walking a few yards in the opposite direction, usually away from home, each time your horse jigs. Stopping and backing your horse a few steps when she jigs may also be effective.

Experiment to find what maneuvers work best for your horse. As with the barn-sour horse, the idea is to refocus her attention on you and show her that it's more work to jig than it is to walk. Remember that releasing the pressure with your hands and legs is

When a horse is jigging, try to refocus her attention by asking her to give her shoulder in one direction for several feet down the trail.

your horse's reward for walking without jigging. Even if she walks nicely for only a few steps, the release of pressure will help teach her that when she complies, she will be rewarded.

Behavior problems aren't fun and can take a lot of work to overcome, but there are many tried-and-true solutions. First, find out whether there's an underlying cause for your horse's behavior. Once health, lifestyle, or basic training issues have been addressed, you can experiment with the on-trail methods detailed above and find what your horse responds to best.

Dangerous Problems

The following behaviors can be quite dangerous, and unless you're an experienced rider, it's advisable to seek the services of a trusted trainer, especially if you're confronted with a horse that bolts, bucks, or rears. Although every horse spooks at something sometimes, a horse that spooks often or violently, or a horse that places you in danger, may need professional training or may not be suitable for trail riding.

Backing Up

Some horses back up rapidly when they're afraid, confused, or refusing your cues. Backing up can become dangerous if your horse chooses to do so into a street or down a gully. When your horse backs up of her own accord, first make sure you're not accidentally telling her to do so. Release all pressure on your reins and legs. If she continues to back up, apply pressure with your legs or give her a firm kick. Use your voice command for going forward, whether it's a kiss, cluck, or "walk on." If none of this works, try turning your horse. Squeeze your fingers and leg on one side—right side for a right bend, left side for a left bend. Pull your hand back toward your hip if you need to, and bump her with your leg to bend her body. Turning your horse will usually stop her from rapidly backing up. Immediately put her to work in a few circles or figures to focus her before moving on.

Bolting

Bolting horses run off when they're frightened. Bolting can be extremely frightening and dangerous. If you're a beginning rider, you should not attempt to solve this problem on your own, especially if your horse has made bolting a habit.

Should your horse bolt, you have several choices based on your comfort level. Sometimes, an immediate and strong reaction can scare the horse, making her want to run off all the more, so a strong, confident rider may choose to let the horse gallop a few strides before stopping her or directing her into a circle. However, most riders don't feel comfortable doing this and prefer to turn the horse into a large circle to slow her down or to use a pulley rein, or one-rein stop. Whatever method you use to stop your horse, remain as calm as possible. Shove your heels down and your legs forward to anchor you in the saddle.

If there's room to do so, turn your horse into a large circle, making the circle smaller and smaller to slow her down. To use a pulley rein, or one-rein stop, slide one hand down a rein to tighten it. Place the opposite hand on the horn or the horse's neck if your saddle doesn't have a horn. Use this arm to brace against as you pull back toward your hip with the opposite hand. Rather than pulling back with both reins, which the bolting horse may brace against, this pulley-rein technique usually will unlock the horse's neck and slow her down while providing the rider with added security. If the horse braces against the pull of the rein, use a give and release, pulling back on the rein for a moment, and then releasing the pressure before pulling back again.

It's almost always easier to turn a bolting horse into a circle to slow her down than it is to stop her straight. However, if there's no room to circle your horse, you'll have to stop her straight. If you can stay secure without holding on, pull back on both reins with a give and release until your horse slows down. Keep your weight in the stirrups. If you need to hold on with one hand, hold one rein tightly in

Turning a bolting horse into a circle or using a pulley rein, as this rider is trying to do, is often more effective than pulling back steadily on both reins.

the hand that's holding the horn, and use a give and release with the other hand.

Bucking

Bucking is a dangerous behavior that can easily unseat the rider. If your horse bucks regularly and you have investigated tack, health issues, diet, and lack of exercise as causes, find a professional trainer to help you overcome this issue.

To buck, a horse must lower her head and shift her weight to her front end, which lightens her hind end enough that she can raise it and kick out. Horses sometimes buck because they're feeling frisky or playful. They may also buck out of pain or fear. If your horse starts to buck or you suspect she's thinking about it, pull her head up and shove your heels down and your legs forward. You can also pull your horse into a tight circle, which will stop her bucking and refocus her attention. If you're going fast when she starts to buck, you may want to use the pulley-rein technique detailed in the bolting section of this chapter. Using a pulley-rein technique to circle your horse will give you the security of one braced hand holding you steady.

Rearing

Rearing is probably the most dangerous of all because a rearing horse can easily lose her balance and flip over on a rider. If your horse rears, do not try to cure this problem on your own. It is far too risky. Hire a trainer. However, if you're caught on a rearing horse, you have to ride it out. As the horse goes up, lean forward and grab a handful of mane. Whatever you do, do not pull back on the reins, or you may pull your horse over on top of you. Once she has all four feet back on the ground, dismount as soon as it's safe.

Spooking

Every horse spooks at one time or another. Horses spook in different ways. Some jump to the side, away from whatever is frightening them; others bolt forward; a few horses even buck or rear; and some stiffen their legs with a jolt that won't throw you but may send your stomach to your knees.

Most horses spook when they're genuinely frightened. You can usually tell when your horse is scared by her body language. She may have wide eyes and flared nostrils, and she may snort or breathe deeply. As we have discussed, never punish a scared horse. It only makes the situation more frightening for her and reinforces her notion that it was bad to begin with. For a horse that's genuinely scared of something, you have a number of ways to approach the situation. You will want to experiment and find the best methods

This rider offers her horse a reassuring pat to help the animal pass a foreign object in the bushes.

based on your horse and the particular circumstances. One option is to stop your horse and let her look at whatever is scaring her—be it a trash can, tarp, or fallen tree—patting her reassuringly and gently encouraging her to move forward and check it out.

You can also use an approach and retreat method—riding toward the scary object, then backing a few steps away from it, resting, and then approaching again. Riders may even choose to dismount and walk their horses up to the scary object to show them it's OK. The benefit of leading your horse is just that: you'll be the leader, and she'll be more likely to approach the scary item. The drawback is that you could get stepped on or knocked over. Make sure your horse leads well, and remember to watch her comfort level, as discussed in chapter 4. If your horse is so scared that she will not respond, try to move past the object rather than approaching it.

On foot, a rider leads her horse past a scary object. This is an option if your horse is well behaved on the lead line.

You may need to make a bit of an arc around the feared item. If you feel comfortable, you can even try pushing your horse into a trot to give her less time to contemplate the object of fear. If you choose to walk or trot past something that's scaring your horse, keep your eyes on the trail ahead, past the object. This will help direct your horse to where you want to go.

Simply moving past the scary object may be the easiest choice for a rare object that you probably won't see again, but you'll want to desensitize your horse to something you need to pass regularly.

To ride past something scary, you can also try tipping your horse's head away from what's frightening her by squeezing the rein on the opposite side of the object or pulling the rein slightly back toward your hip. Use your leg on the same side as the squeezing rein to keep the horse moving forward. The goal is to get your horse to look away from the scary item without actually moving her entire body away from it. Sometimes circling your horse several times in each direction can also help her refocus on you and away from what's scaring her.

Experiment to find what works best and what is safest given your particular circumstances. Remember that you are the herd leader. Keep your nerves in check. Take a deep breath and relax. Guide your horse with confidence so she can put her trust in you. If you speak to her, do so in a reassuring and confident voice.

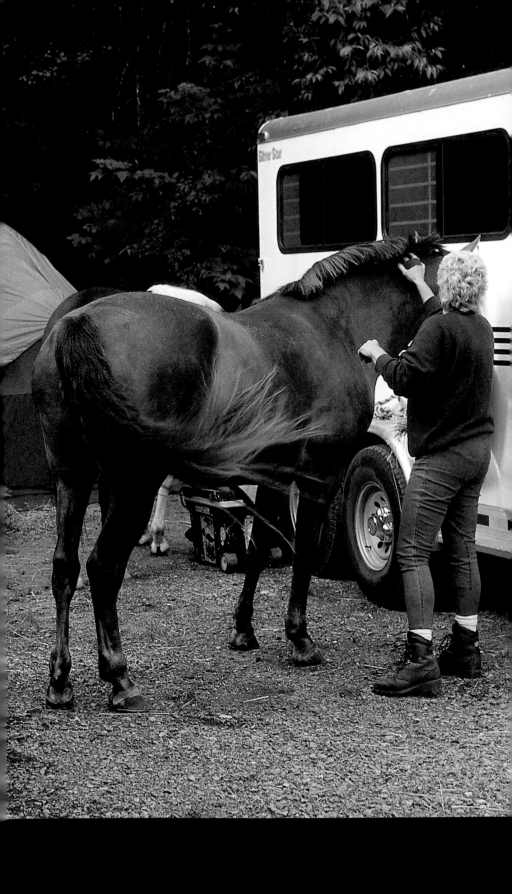

8

Going Places with Your Horse

Now comes the fun part, when all of your careful preparation pays off, and you're ready to hit the trails. There are many ways to enjoy trail riding with your horse: you can search out new trails that are accessible from your home, explore a little farther by trailering out for day rides, go camping for days, or trail ride with fellow enthusiasts on an organized ride.

Finding Trails in Your Area

There's nothing like walking out your back door and going for a trail ride. Unfortunately, trails are dwindling virtually everywhere as urban sprawl and development take over and private landowners, often afraid of lawsuits, prohibit equestrians from riding on their land. However, there are still many wonderful trails for the taking.

If you keep your horse at home, you may already be familiar with most of the trails in your area. But don't think there aren't undiscovered gems nearby. Talk to other equestrians, joggers, and hikers in your surrounding area. Often, with a little ingenuity, you can find routes to new trails, nearby state or national parks, or large expanses of land. Finding these trails may mean you have to cut through a neighborhood or even an industrial zone (which are usually quiet on the weekends), but if you have a calm, well-behaved horse, these routes can be a viable option for finding new trails.

A group of riders fords a stream side by side. Lessen your impact on sensitive habitats by riding single file.

Everyone who enjoys trails should take an active role in maintaining and protecting them or face losing them in the future.

Protecting Local Trails

There are many ways you can become involved in preserving trails. First, ride conscientiously. Try to always stay on the trail. If an area is sensitive because of mud, ride at a walk and single file to avoid disrupting the ground further. Ride single file at a walk as well through water crossings, and don't let your horse eliminate near lakes and streams. Never tie your horse near a water source, as this will damage and erode the sensitive habitat. When tying your horse on trail, use designated tie areas whenever possible. If you must tie to a tree, use a special tree-saver tie. For your horse's safety, tie him high to a healthy, sturdy tree.

Second, follow the rules and be polite; don't give anyone a reason to ban horses from an area. If you will be riding across private land, try to get the owner's permission. Many property owners are hesitant to allow horses on their property because they're worried a

By a mountain stream, a rider takes a break from the trail, after securely tying his horse to a sturdy evergreen tree.

horse or rider will get injured and try to hold the property owner liable, so offer to sign a liability release. Whenever you ride across someone's land, leave any gates as you found them. Heed signs that indicate equestrians are prohibited from a certain area or that no trespassers are allowed. Never let your horse walk on a farmer's crops or on flowers or other sensitive landscaping (and don't let your horse grab bites of these things, either).

Last, become active in the local trail community. If trails are in jeopardy in your area, find out what's being done to save them. Even if the trails aren't being threatened by development, volunteer to help clean and maintain them. June is national outdoors month, which features National Trails Day, a great opportunity to get involved. You can also work to organize trail cleanup or maintenance days on your own or ask park rangers at your local state or national park how you can help. There are also national organizations, such as the Equestrian Land Conservation Resource, that work to educate people and preserve trails.

Sharing Trails

Some of your best allies in protecting and preserving local trails may be hikers, mountain bikers, and other cyclists. Wherever you ride, you're bound to run into these groups. Although bikers and equestrians have often been at odds when it comes to trail use (some equestrians have even been hit by speeding bikes), it's best to learn to share the trails peacefully.

State and national parks will usually indicate which trails are open to equestrians and bikers and will post signs that indicate that horses have the right-of-way. Most equestrians assume horses have the right-of-way, but not all hikers and bikers are aware of this. In addition, mountain bikers often whiz downhill and may not see you as they come around a corner. If there's space for you to move easily out of a biker's way, do so. You can also call to the biker to slow down, horse ahead. Always use a friendly tone, and thank bikers or hikers who stop or move aside to let you pass. Desensitize your horse to bikes at home before going out on trail to ensure your horse won't get too worked up when you encounter bikes. (See chapter 4 for more information on desensitization.)

Trailering Out for Day Rides

If you don't have endless trails right outside your back door, there are likely great trail riding opportunities within a short driving distance. State, national, and city parks often allow equestrians, and many even feature staging areas where you can park your truck and trailer. Ask around, then visit these locations without your horse first so you know exactly what kind of trails and terrain to expect. Of course, you'll need a horse trailer to go out on day rides, or you can plan the ride with a friend who has a horse trailer.

Preparations

Never plan to go somewhere without first knowing whether your horse loads into and out of the trailer easily. If he doesn't, you'll need to work on this several months in advance. There are many methods for teaching a horse to load. If your horse has a strong aversion to trailers, you may need to hire a professional trainer to help teach him to load. (Make sure you're comfortable with the trainer's methods.)

Whichever method you or the trainer uses, the most important rule to follow is *never* whip or force the horse into the trailer. You want him to load calmly and quietly in the future, and forcing him into the trailer even once will only strengthen his notion that it's a scary and stressful event. Never load your horse unless the trailer is securely attached to the tow vehicle and the tires are blocked. If you

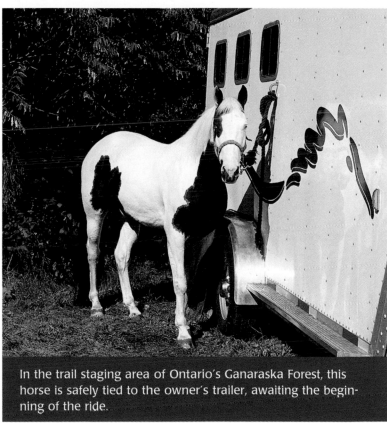

In the trail staging area of Ontario's Ganaraska Forest, this horse is safely tied to the owner's trailer, awaiting the beginning of the ride.

do so, the trailer could shift or begin to roll with the added weight of a horse.

Once you have a destination picked out and your horse and rig are ready to travel, plan your ride with your horse's fitness and abilities in mind. If the area you'll be riding in features a different type of terrain than your horse is used to, such as steep hills, you may need to keep your ride shorter and your pace slower than usual. If there are water crossings, make sure ahead of time that your horse is comfortable crossing water. Take into account that new sights and sounds, such as motorboats on a lake, may spook him. Most horses will be more excited when trailering out to an

A woman longes her draft horse. You can longe your horse for fifteen or twenty minutes or turn him out at home before trailering out for a day ride.

unfamiliar location than they are at home, so make sure your horse is longed or turned out before you load him, and don't attempt a ride away from home if your horse hasn't been ridden in several days and may be extra frisky.

You'll also need to thoroughly check your trailer before you load up for your day ride. Make sure the lights and brakes are working, the floorboards are in good repair, and all the tires are properly inflated. It's advisable to carry two spare tires and emergency road flares when trailering.

Feed your horse before you leave on your journey. If you place feed in the trailer, make sure it's not too dusty, which can bother your horse's respiratory system. Hay can be wetted down before it's placed in the trailer. If your trailer doesn't have a feed manger built in, you can leave your horse untied and place the hay at his feet if it's safe to do so, or you can hang a hay bag high enough that he can't get his front feet hung up on it. However, if you're driving only a short distance and your horse is a good traveler, you may want to forgo the feed in transit.

What to Take

Trailering out for a day ride also requires a bit of extra preparation. The following are some items you'll need for your journey:

Protection: Use leg wraps or shipping boots to protect your horse's legs in the trailer. A head bumper to protect the top of his head should he jerk it up on his way in or out of the trailer is also advisable. A blanket for the trailer ride will also be necessary if it's cold out, as wind chill can be a factor on the road.

Water: Many horses don't like to drink "strange" water, so always bring plenty of water from home for your horse to drink before and after his ride unless you know there's a reliable water source at your destination and your horse will drink. Bring extra water on hot days, not only because your horse will drink more but also to sponge him down after the ride.

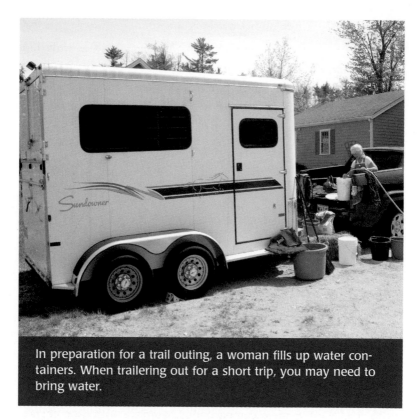

In preparation for a trail outing, a woman fills up water containers. When trailering out for a short trip, you may need to bring water.

Hay: Some parks allow only weed-free hay on the premises, so call ahead. Weed-free hay is sometimes required to prevent the introduction of weeds into the habitat.

Pooper-scooper: A pooper-scooper to clean up after your horse at the staging area is a must. Be appreciative of the facilities and opportunity to ride there, and always clean up after yourself and your horse.

Usual trail essentials: In addition to these extra items, pack all your usual trail essentials, as outlined in chapter 5. If you're riding in an unfamiliar location, pay attention to each turn you take, carry a map, and consider a compass or GPS as an added measure.

Upon Arrival

Once you reach the staging area, unload your horse and walk him around a bit. Most trailers have tie rings on them so you can tie your horse as you groom and tack him up. Whenever and wherever you tie your horse, he should be able to hold his head in a natural position, but always tie him short and high enough that he can't get tangled in the rope or get his head under it or a leg over it. As always, use a quick release knot when tying your horse, and make sure the trailer is still attached to the tow vehicle, with its tires securely blocked.

Secure any valuables under lock and key before you hit the trail, and remember to pick up a park map if one is available. Whenever you're riding in a new place, keep track of what trails and turns you're taking so you can find your way back!

Camping with Your Horse

Camping with your horse may conjure images of tents, packhorses, and tie lines, but if you pick the right destination, you won't need to worry about tying or hobbling your horse for the night. You can even bring your RV if you have one. Many private, state, and national parks offer horse campgrounds complete with pipe corrals, running water, and RV hookups. You can find these locations by looking online, buying guidebooks, or making some phone calls. (See the Resources section.)

Before You Go

Plan ahead because many horse campgrounds fill up well in advance; you'll most likely need reservations. Find out exactly what the facility provides and its rules and regulations (such as weed-free hay). Pack your horse's meals, plus some additional feed "just in case." If you need to change your horse's feed for the trip—for instance, from hay to pellet horse feed or to a different type of hay— begin any feed change gradually over several weeks.

A rider tacks up while a companion patiently awaits his owner at the stabling area in New York's Otter Creek State Park.

You'll need to pack a large container to hold your horse's water in the campground corral. It will probably be hard to pack enough water for your horse to last a weekend, so make sure your horse is comfortable drinking "different" water. If he's a very finicky drinker, you may have to get him used to drinking flavored water (flavoring can disguise the taste of foreign water), but begin this process many weeks ahead of time. Apple juice is one possible flavoring that can be added to a horse's water trough. A few drops of peppermint are also a possibility. Another option for a finicky horse is to try mixing your home water with the water at the campground to get him used to it.

Pack all the same gear outlined above for a day ride, plus your own camping gear and a complete first aid kit for your horse and another for you. If the campground is out of range for your regular veterinarian, locate one in the new area ahead of time in case of emergency. Ask your veterinarian for a referral, talk to fellow horse owners, or contact the American Association of Equine Practitioners (http://www.myhorsematters.com). Write down the names and numbers of several veterinarians, then call to make sure they would treat your horse if you have an emergency in their area.

If you're traveling out of state, you'll need to carry your horse's Coggins test and a Certificate of Veterinary Inspection or health certificate. A negative Coggins test is required for interstate transit. A Coggins test looks for equine infectious anemia, a contagious and incurable disease. A health certificate is signed by your veterinarian stating that your horse does not show signs of disease. Health certificates are generally valid only for a limited time, and some states have specific rules for what constitutes a valid Coggins or health certificate, so research the rules in your state and any state you plan to travel to. Also, make sure your horse is up to date on his vaccinations. If he's traveling to an area where different diseases may be a concern, ask your veterinarian whether additional shots are necessary. Also bring proof of ownership, such as pictures of you with the horse and any microchip or registration information in case your horse is lost or stolen.

Make sure your horse's feet are in good repair before you go camping. Don't wait until the end of your horse's shoeing or trimming cycle, as this will make loose shoes or cracks more likely. If necessary, though, ask a local veterinarian to refer you to a farrier should your horse lose a shoe or have another foot problem while you're camping.

During the Drive

If your camping destination is several hours away, you'll need to give your horse's comfort during transit a great deal of thought. Pack various blankets to outfit your horse as the weather changes. For example, he may need a heavy blanket if it's cold when you start out, but as the day warms up you'll want to switch to a lighter blanket. Even if he never wears a blanket at home, the windchill factor in a trailer can make one necessary when it's cool out.

As you drive, allow more room than usual between your rig and the vehicle in front of you because it takes longer to stop with a horse trailer. Always stop slowly and make your turns carefully.

Always outfit your horse in shipping boots (as shown here) to protect his legs during transit.

Remember that your horse cannot see a stop or turn coming to prepare for it, so keep his situation in mind. Standing in a trailer and bracing for turns and stops is a lot of work for a horse—it's not restful, so stop every couple of hours and let your horse stand and relax in the trailer. If your horse loads easily, and you've found a quiet grassy area, you can unload him and offer him water. He should be offered water at least every four hours on a long trip.

Horses need to lower their heads to clear their lungs, so if it's safe to do so, you can leave your horse untied during transit. If you do tie him, use a tie with a quick release snap on the end that attaches to the trailer. Either way, undo his lead rope so it doesn't get tangled on his legs or any part of the trailer. As mentioned above, check your trailer thoroughly before you load up, pack the appropriate emergency gear, and be considerate about what and how you feed your horse in the trailer.

At Your Destination

For both your health and your horse's, consider your destination. If you're traveling into high-altitude areas, you and your horse will need several days to acclimate, or you'll have to keep your rides shorter and easier than you do at lower altitudes. When traveling into the desert to ride, remember to tailor your rides according to the heat and possibly deep, sandy footing. As always, hot weather necessitates more frequent water breaks for your horse, so don't plan long rides on routes that do not have drinking water available for your horse.

Remember to tell someone where you're going and how long you'll be gone when you leave for a trail ride. Pick up a map of the trails if one is available, and pay attention to the route you're taking so you can retrace your steps if needed. Be courteous and clean up after yourself and your horse at the campsite, and always put any trash back in your saddlebags if trash cans are not available along the trail.

At an overnight camp in Ontario's Sandaraska Park, an endurance competitor enjoys dinner in a portable pen.

Camping with your horse is a great way to explore our nation's fabulous parks and see some spectacular sights. If you're properly prepared, it can be a relaxing and inexpensive vacation. If camping isn't your cup of tea, there are even some bed, barn, and breakfast inns around the country that can accommodate you and your horse near great trails. For more information on finding places to camp or stay with your horse, see the Resources section of this book.

Joining a Trail Riding Group

Where there are horses, there are trail riding groups. Even if you live in a small town, there may be one in the next city over, or you can organize your own! There may be a small membership fee. Some local groups are part of larger nationwide organizations, such as the Back Country Horseman. Groups may organize rides weekly, monthly, or semiannually. They may organize day rides or weekend campouts or fun competitions, such as poker rides.

Joining a trail riding group can have many benefits, including making friends and finding new trails. With a little looking, you can find a group that's a good fit. Some groups will be mostly older riders, others younger or a mix, and certain groups will be serious, whereas others are out to party and have a good time. Once you locate a group, ask if you can go on a ride or volunteer to help with a ride before joining (if there's a membership fee). This will allow you to see if the group is right for you.

The best way to find a group near you is to ask around. Inquire at the feed store and ask fellow horsemen in your area, including your veterinarian and farrier. Local riding clubs that put on horse shows may also have a trail riding group. In addition, check out the Resources section of this book.

Planned Rides

Planned rides are different from trail riding groups in that they are a one-time sponsored group ride. They're often put on by local riding clubs, including trail riding groups and organizations, and they usually have a small fee associated with them (which may include a meal). Riding clubs, groups and organizations also put on benefit planned trail rides, where the donation or ride fee goes to a designated charity.

Breed associations, including the American Paint Horse Association and the American Quarter Horse Association, sponsor

Joining a local trail riding group such as this one is a great way to meet fellow trail riders and to explore new trails in your area.

many trail rides each year. You usually do not need to be a member or ride a registered horse to participate. However, most breed associations offer points programs for members; the more hours in the saddle you log, the more prizes you receive.

Planned rides are often day rides, but weekend rides are common as well. Participating in a planned ride offers similar benefits to joining a riding group—the chance to meet like-minded individuals and explore new countryside.

At some point in your trail riding career, you may yearn for a bit of competition, and trail riding offers many choices. Here are a few options:

- Poker rides are basically organized group rides with a poker hand thrown in.

- Trail trials, or judged pleasure rides, are half-day or day-long trail rides with judged obstacles along the way.

- Competitive trail rides cover 25 to 90 miles, at speeds between 3.5 and 6 mph. Riders are judged on their presentation, grooming, trail equitation, trail safety and courtesy, and stabling, while horses are judged on their condition, soundness, and ability over natural obstacles.

- Endurance rides range from 25 to 100 miles, over one or two days, and the rider who completes the course first and who passes all the vet checks wins.

- Ride and tie matches two riders and one horse in a long-distance ride, racing against other teams. Riders alternate riding and running.

- Mounted orienteering is a competitive sport that pits groups of riders or individual riders against each other in a type of treasure hunt.

With so many options available, you'll be loading up your horse and exploring new trails in no time. All you need is a horse, a trailer, and a bit of preparation.

Resources

The following are resources for finding trails, competitions, camping locations, lodging, planned rides, and trail riding groups:

American Endurance Ride Conference
PO Box 6027
Auburn, CA 95604
866-271-AERC
http://www.aerc.org
Straight from the source: "The American Endurance Ride Conference (AERC) was founded in 1972 as a national governing body for long-distance riding."

American Quarter Horse Association
1600 Quarter Horse Dr.
Amarillo, TX 79104
806-376-4811
http://www.aqha.org
Straight from the source: "Since 1997, more than 46,000 riders have traveled through scenic canyons, ridden across snow-capped mountains, and strolled horseback along sunny beaches through AQHA's Ride Program."

American Trail Horse Association
PO Box 293
Cortland, IL 60112
877-266 1678

http://www.trailhorse.com
Straight from the source: "ATHA is dedicated to the registration, education, identification, certification, and acknowledgment of the American Trail Horse, regardless of color, breed, size, or bloodlines."

American Trails
PO Box 491797
Redding, CA 96049-1797
530-547-2060
http://www.americantrails.org
Straight from the source: "Our members are working to enhance and protect America's growing network of interconnected trails. We support local, regional, and long-distance greenways and trails, whether in backcountry, rural, or urban areas."

Back Country Horsemen of America
PO Box 1367
Graham WA 98338-1367
888-893-5161
http://www.backcountryhorse
.com
Straight from the source: "Back Country Horsemen of America is a nonprofit corporation made up of state organizations, affiliates, and at-large members. We are dedicated to preserving the his-

torical use of recreational stock in the back country commensurate with our heritage."

Bed & Breakfast Inns ONLINE
PO Box 829
Madison, TN 37116
800-215-7365
http://www.bbonline.com
Straight from the source: "Locate a bed and breakfast inn with accommodations for horses."

California State Horsemen's Association
264 Clovis Ave., Ste. 109
Clovis, CA 93612
559-325-1055
http://www.californiastatehorsemen.com
Straight from the source: "Incorporated in 1942, the California State Horsemen's Association comprises twenty geographical regions within three areas (Northern, Central, and Southern). CSHA represents the pleasure-horse industry and pleasure-horse owners."

Equestrian Land Conservation Resource
4041 Iron Works Pkwy
Lexington, KY 40511
859-233-4303
http://www.elcr.org
Straight from the source: "Loss of open land has been identified as the greatest threat to the future of all equestrian sport, recreation, and industry. By educating horse people and encouraging partnerships with conservationists and other user groups at the local level, the Equestrian Land Conservation Resource is mobilizing thousands of equestrians to work for land access and protection in their communities."

Equestrian Trails, Inc.
13741 Foothill Blvd., Ste. 100
Sylmar, CA 91342-3143
818-362-6819
http://www.etinational.com
Straight from the source: "Equestrian Trails, Inc. was established as a nonprofit corporation in 1944 with the Charter to be 'Dedicated to the Acquisition and Preservation of Trails, Good Horsemanship, and Equine Legislation.' We are a family-oriented riding club based in Sylmar, Calif."

Horse & Mule Trail Guide USA
http://www.horseandmuletrails.com
Straight from the source: "This Web site is a collection of trails and places to camp and ride submitted by trail riders."

Horse Motels International
PO Box 230373
Las Vegas, NV 89105

702-622-0026
http://horsemotel.com
From the source: "We offer a complete listing by country, province, and state of horse motels anywhere in the world. If you're traveling and need lodging for your horse(s), check our Web site for a facility along your way."

Horse Trails and Campgrounds
http://www.horsetraildirectory.com
From the source: "We hope you will find some great trail riding and horse camping places that have been described by others, and we invite you to share your experiences by rating trails and adding trails and campgrounds to this trail riders' database."

Horse Trails Coast to Coast: The Traveler's Guide to Great Riding Getaways
by Vicki Hogue-Davies
BowTie Press, a Division of BowTie, Inc.
Irvine, California
http://www.bowtiepress.com
From the source: "Horse Trails reveals the most interesting and appealing riding venues in the United States. Each area's trails are rated by difficulty, so you'll be able to tell at a glance if you want to saddle up or move along. You'll also learn the inside scoop on the best places to stable your horse and your-

self, where to eat, and what sites to visit after a day on the trails."

HorseTrip.com
http://www.horsetrip.com
From the source: "Welcome to HorseTrip.com, featuring a state-by-state directory of stables, horse motels, equine-friendly camping, and bed and breakfasts that will stable your horse after a long day on the road."

Interactive Outdoors, Inc.
312 AABC, Ste. D
Aspen, CO 81611
800-741-1717
http://www.wildernet.com
From the source: "Truly an interactive site, Wildernet.com allows you to search for recreation information by activity type or specific geographic area. We encourage you to share your experiences with fellow users by posting trip reports and comments. We also invite rangers and other outdoor professionals to update local conditions."

Long Riders' Guild
http://www.thelongridersguild.com
From the source: "Part museum, book store, tack room, and Guild Hall, this Web site contains the world's largest collection of equestrian travel information."

National Association of
Competitive Mounted
Orienteering
http://www.nacmo.org
From the source: "CMO is like a
mounted treasure hunt, which tests
your horsemanship, your map-
reading ability, and your compass
skills—all while having great fun
with your horse!"

National Park Service
http://www.nps.gov;
http://www.recreation.gov
Straight from the source: "Today,
many of our parks, forests, and
wilderness areas can still be
explored on the back of a horse for
a unique natural adventure. Many
federal recreation areas offer trail
riding as well as off-trail riding."

**National Recreation Reservation
Service**
877-444-6777
http://www.reserveusa.com
From the source: "The NRRS
is a one-stop reservation service
for the USDA Forest Service, Army
Corps of Engineers, National Park
Service, Bureau of Land
Management, and Bureau of
Reclamation outdoor recreation
facilities and activities. With over
45,000 reservable facilities at over
1,700 locations, the NRRS is the
largest outdoor recreation reservation service in the country."

**North American Trail Ride
Conference**
PO Box 224
Sedalia, CO 80135
303-688-1677
http://www.natrc.org
Straight from the source:
"NATRC is one of a number of
competitive trail ride organizations in the United States. A competitive trail ride is not a race,
but competitors cover a marked
course in a given period of time."

The Ride and Tie Association
PO Box 835
Alpine, CA 91903
619-445-4485
http://www.rideandtie.org
Straight from the source:
"Although the sport of ride and tie
has been in existence since 1971, it
is a relatively unknown sport that
combines trail running, endurance
riding and most of all, strategy. The
object is to get all three team members (two humans and one horse)
across a 20- to 100-mile cross-
country course by alternating riding
and running."

TrailSource
http://www.trailsource.com
From the source: "The
Horseback Riding TrailSource is
your online adventure guide to
the best horse trails and trail
rides around the globe!"

Glossary

aids: Natural aids include using the hands, legs, voice, and seat to cue the horse. Artificial aids include the use of a crop or spurs.

antigrazing reins: A device that runs from the saddle to the horse's bridle and prevents the horse from lowering his head enough to graze.

barn-sour: A horse that doesn't want to leave the barn or tries to rush home to the barn.

bars of the mouth: The area in a horse's mouth where no teeth grow, between the front teeth and the back teeth. The bit rests on the bars of a horse's mouth.

borium: The common name for tungsten carbide. Borium can be added to the bottom of a horse's shoes for extra traction, especially during winter riding.

body clip: Shaving the horse's entire body for show or for easier cooling out in the winter.

bowed tendon: An injury to a tendon in the horse's legs that "bows" out, creating a puffy area on the leg.

breast collar: A leather or synthetic strap that connects to both sides of the saddle and runs in front of the horse's chest to help steady the saddle and keep it from sliding back.

bridle: Usually refers to the headstall, bit, and reins.

browband: A strap on the bridle that runs across the horse's forehead above his eyes.

buck: When a horse lowers his head, puts his weight on his front end, and kicks out with his hind legs.

calks (or studs): Grips (like cleats) attached to the bottom of the horse's shoe to prevent slipping on certain surfaces.

canter: A three-beat gait that is faster than a trot, in which the horse starts off the footfall sequence on one of his hind legs, for example the right hind leg, then the left hind leg and front right leg move together, and finally the left front, or leading leg, lands. The canter is equivalent to the western lope, only slightly faster.

cantle: The back part of a saddle that rises behind the seat.

chair seat: A position flaw in which the rider has his or her legs too far in front, rather than having the heels in line with the hips.

chin strap or chain, also called a curb strap or chain: A leather or synthetic strap or metal chain that runs under the horse's chin—commonly used with leverage bits.

cinch: The wide strap on a western saddle that goes around the horse's girth area and is tightened until snug to hold the saddle on.

conformation: The way a horse is put together, including the angles of his bones. A horse with poor conformation may have crooked legs or other flaws that impair his physical ability and soundness.

crupper: A strap that runs from the back of the saddle around the dock of the horse's tail and helps steady the saddle and keep it from sliding forward.

cues: Directions the rider gives the horse with his or her hands, legs, voice, and seat.

curb bit: A leverage bit with shanks that features a port, or curve, in the mouthpiece.

desensitize: A process that involves exposing the horse to stimuli, such as objects he fears, in a safe environment so he will not overreact when he sees them in a noncontrolled environment.

diagonal: When a rider is posting or rising with the horse's motion at the trot, the rider is on either the left or the right diagonal, meaning he or she rises with the right front and left hind pair of legs or with the left front and right hind pair of legs.

direct pressure bit: A bit such as a snaffle that works directly on the horse's mouth, without amplifying the pressure from the rider's hands.

dismounting: When the rider gets off of the horse's back and stands on the ground.

dock: The top part of a horse's tail, where it connects to the rest of his body.

electrolytes: Powder or paste mineral supplements that can be added to a horse's diet or given in an emergency situation, as recommended by a veterinarian.

equitation: Proper riding, or a rider's form.

farrier: A professional trained in hoof trimming or shoeing or both.

flanks: The sensitive area on the lower back part of a horse's belly.

floating: When a horse has the sharp edges on his teeth filed down by a veterinarian.

gait: A horse's movement or speed, such as the walk, the trot, the canter, and the gallop.

gaited horse: A horse with additional gaits or gaits other than the walk, the trot, the canter, and the gallop.

girth: The wide strap on an English saddle that is tightened until snug to hold the saddle in place. It also refers to the part of the horse's body on his rib cage behind his front legs.

ground pole: A rounded board, usually several inches in diameter and several feet long, used for horses to walk over.

gullet: The front, rounded, open area of the saddle below the pommel and above the horse's withers.

halter: A head collar used for leading and tying the horse.

headstall: A head collar used for holding the bit (or hackamore) in place.

high line: A line secured high for tying horses to on the trail or when camping without corrals.

hobble: A device that goes around the horse's front ankles, or pasterns, to make it hard for him to walk off—often used when camping overnight or for grazing breaks in unfenced areas.

horn: The "handle" that rises out of the pommel on a western saddle, a trail saddle, and an Australian stock saddle.

jigging: A bouncy movement when a nervous horse is neither walking nor jogging.

jog: The western equivalent of a trot, which is slower than the trot but is also a two-beat gait, in which the opposite front and hind legs move together.

lame: Usually refers to a horse that is limping on one or more of his legs.

leverage bit: Bits that work off pressure placed on the horse's port, pole, chin, bars, and possibly tongue. Leverage bits include curb bits, pelhams, kimberwicks, and Tom Thumbs.

longe line: A long line or rope used for longeing a horse, in which the handler asks the horse to move in large circles around him or her.

lope: A three-beat gait faster than a jog. The footfall sequence is as follows: the horse starts off with one of his hind legs, for example the right hind leg; next, the left hind leg and front right leg move together; and finally the left front, or leading leg, lands. The lope is the equivalent of the English canter, only slower.

mechanical hackamore: A device used instead of a bit. It controls the horse via pressure on his nose, the chin strap or curb chain, and his poll.

mounting: Getting up onto the horse's back.

mouthpiece: The part of a bit that goes in the horse's mouth. Mouthpieces vary in material, width, and shape.

navicular: The navicular bone is a small bone in the horse's hoof. When a horse has problems with this bone or in that area, he is often said to have navicular, navicular syndrome, or navicular disease and will usually be lame or intermittently lame.

neck reining: As opposed to direct reining, in which the rider pulls on the bit and rides with one hand on each rein; in neck reining, the rider rides with both reins in one hand. When the rider wants the horse to turn, he or she moves the rein hand in the direction of the turn. The opposite rein then touches the horse's neck and tells him to turn. A horse must be trained to neck rein.

pommel: The front of the saddle that rises up. On a western saddle and on some trail saddles and Australian stock saddles, the pommel is the part of the saddle the horn is attached to.

posting: When a rider moves with the horse's trot, rising slightly out of the saddle and forward with either the right or left diagonal.

pulley rein: When a rider holds on to the horse's mane or the saddle horn with one hand and pulls back hard with the other rein to stop the horse or make the horse turn in a circle and slow down.

rearing: When a horse shifts his weight to his hind end and lifts his front end and legs into the air.

reins: Leather, synthetic, or rope straps that attach to the bit and go to the rider's hands for steering and control.

ringbone: An arthritic condition in which hard, bony ridges form near the horse's fetlock area. Ringbone is usually classified as high or low ringbone and can cause lameness.

saddlebags: Bags made of leather or synthetic materials that attach to the saddle and allow the rider to carry things out on a ride.

saddle bars: Part of the frame of the saddle. Made of wood or synthetic material, the bars run along either side of the horse's spine.

saddle fender: The wide leather or synthetic flaps on a western, a trail, or an Australian stock saddle to which the stirrups attach and that run between the rider's inner legs and the horse.

saddle skirt: The part of a western or a trail saddle behind and below the seat, above the horse's flank. Skirts are generally squared off in shape or rounded.

saddletree: The frame of a saddle that determines its width.

side-pass: When the horse walks sideways, crossing his legs.

snaffle: A bit that works off direct pressure rather than leverage. A snaffle can be straight (meaning the mouthpiece has no joints), jointed, or have a link in the middle of the joints.

snow pads: Pads that are placed in a horse's shoes during the winter to prevent snow from balling up in his hooves.

sound: When a horse is healthy and travels normally without a limp or pain.

splint: When a horse has "a splint," it refers to a little hard bump on the splint bone, which is in a horse's lower leg, below his knee or hock, near his large cannon bone. A splint may be accompanied by pain and swelling. This can be caused by something striking the splint bone, such as the horse's other hoof or a hard object. Splint boots can help protect the splint bone when riding.

spook: When a horse is frightened by something and jumps sideways, bolts, or makes a sudden movement.

stirrup: The part of a saddle where you put the ball of your foot.

stride: Refers to the sequence of steps in a particular gait. The length of stride is judged from where one hoof lifts up to where that same hoof sets down.

sweep rider: A rider who brings up the rear on a group trail ride and makes sure no one is left behind.

tack: The equipment a rider uses on a horse, including the saddle, bridle, and breast collar.

throatlatch: The strap on a bridle that goes under the horse's throat and buckles near his cheek.

Tom Thumb bit: A bit with a mouthpiece that resembles a snaffle and shanks that make it a leverage bit.

trail bell: A bell that can be attached to a horse's breast collar or saddle to ring and warn wild animals, such as bears, that something is approaching.

tree saver: A strap that goes around a tree without being abrasive so a rider can tie a horse without harming the tree.

trot: The English equivalent of a jog, only faster. The trot is also a two-beat gait, in which the opposite front and hind legs move together.

turn on forehand: A tight turn in which the horse rotates his front feet, keeping them almost in the same spot, while his hind end moves around in a partial or complete turn.

turn on haunches: A tight turn in which the horse rotates his hind feet, keeping them almost in the same spot, while his front end moves around to make a partial or complete turn.

withers: The bone at the end of a horse's neck that usually rises up in a half circle.

Index

A

adult seat sizes, 40
age versus temperament, training, and
  health, 15–16
aids: food as, 146, 149, 161–62; seat,
  66–68; tack-based, 54; voice as,
  72. See also cues, hand and leg
altitude considerations, 19, 187
American Association of Equine
  Practitioners, 184
American Paint Horses, 21
American Quarter Horses, 21–22
American Society for Testing and
  Materials (ASTM), 61
Andalusians, 28
animal threats, 122–23, 123–25
antigrazing reins, 162
Appaloosas, 22
approach-and-retreat for scary
  objects, 172
Arabians, 22, 23
arm position while riding, 71
arthritis, 19
ASTM (American Society for Testing
  and Materials), 61
ASTM/SEI-approved helmets, 60, 61
attire, 59–61
attributes of a trail horse, 11, 13–14
Australian stock saddles, 36, 39

B

Back Country Horseman, 188
backing: controlled, 78–79, 92;
  uncontrolled, 167
back problems of horse, 19, 112
bad habits, remediating, 153. See also
  trainers
balance, importance of, 63–64
bareback trail riding, 39
barn-sour horses, 157–62
bars of the mouth, 46, 49
bars of the saddle, 40, 43
bear country, 124
bees, 123
behavior problems: about, 151, 157,
  167; backing up randomly, 167;
  barn-sour horses, 157–62; bolting,
  168–70; bucking, 170; grass grabbing, 162, 163; head tossing,
  162–64; jigging, 141, 164–67; from

misfit saddle, 43; prevention technique, 155–57; rearing, 170; reasons
  for, 151–55; spooking, 170–73
bell boots, 58–59
bits: about, 44;
direct pressure bits, 44–46, 50, 51; fitting, 47–49, 152; leverage bits, 44,
  45, 46–47, 50, 70–71; riding technique, 70–71
black bears, 124
blankets for trailer ride, 181, 185
body clip, 126
body language, horse's, 155
bolting behavior, 168–70
boots for horses: bell boots, 58–59;
  hoof boots, 110, 120; shipping
  boots, 181; splint or sport boots,
  58–59, 122
boots for riders, 59, 60
borium, 111
bowed tendon, 19, 195
branches over trail, 78
breast collars, 56, 57
breed associations, 190
breeds: about, 20, 25; American Paint
  Horses, 21; American Quarter
  Horses, 21–22; Andalusians, 28;
  Appaloosas, 22; Arabians, 22, 23;
  gaited breeds, 25–27, 29;
  Morgans, 22; Mustangs, 23;
  Standardbreds, 24;
  Thoroughbreds, 24, 25
bridles: about, 44; bit fit, 47–49, 152;
  bit types, 44–47, 50, 70–71; halter bridle combinations, 44, 50;
  headstalls, 49–52. See also bits
browband headstalls, 49–50
buckets, collapsible, 121, 129–30
bucking behavior, 170
buying trail horses, 20, 29–33, 154

C

calks for snow conditions, 111
calm demeanor, 13
camping, 183–88
canter, 196
cantle, 196
cavessons, 50
cell phone, carrying a, 119, 149
cement, riding on, 106

Certificate of Veterinary Inspection, 185
chair seat, 66, 67
chin straps, 46, 47, 50
cinches, 39–40, 43–44
"cinchy" horses, 43
clean legs, 19
clothing for riding, 59–61
Coggins test, 185
colic, 131
collapsible bucket, packing a, 121, 129–30
compass, carrying a, 121
competitive trail riding, 117–18, 190
conditioning program, 115–18
conformation, 17, 20. *See also specific breeds*
connected western reins, 52, 53
consistency, importance of, 154, 157, 160
cooling out, 133–35
corrals, training for lack of, 15
cruppers, 56, 58
cues, hand and leg: for backing up, 78–79; as basic skill, 14; consistency of, 154; controlling grass grabbers, 162; distracting a fidgety horse with, 138, 141, 146, 158–59, 165–67; give and release, 168–70; hand equitation, 68–71; inexperienced horses, 14–15, 152; inexperienced riders, 14, 152–53; leg equitation, 64–66; for obstacles on trail, 77–80, 90–91; pulley rein, 168–70; for scary objects on trail, 172–73; for side-passing, 80; for speeding up and slowing down, 66, 141–42; with spurs, 54; for stopping rapid backups, 167. *See also* equitation
curb bits, 44, 45, 46, 50, 70
curb straps, 46, 47, 50
curiosity, horse's, 13–14

D
deer hunting season, 59
dehydration, 126–31
desensitization: about, 87, 101, 106–7; approach-and-retreat method, 172; to human activities, 102, 178; to obstacles on trail, 90–93; to other animals, 101–2; preparation for, 87–88; for riding alone, 145–49; to scary objects, 93–98, 171–73;

to trail gear, 88–89; to vehicles, 102–6; for water crossings, 98–101
diagonals while posting, 67–68
diet, effects of, 154–55
direct pressure bits, 44–46, 50, 51, 70–71
dismounting, 74
dock, 197
dog desensitization, 102
dogs on trail, 123–24
draw reins, 54
driving with a trailer, 185–86
duct tape, packing, 121

E
ear bonnets, 114
electrolytes, 116, 197
emergencies on trail, 30, 184
endurance racing, 117–18, 190
endurance saddles, 36, 37, 39
English headstalls, 50, 51
English reins, 53
English saddles, 39, 40
environment: horse's preference, 11; protecting the, 176–78, 187
EpiPen, carrying a, 123
equine heart-rate monitors, 117–18
equipment: packing for the trail, 88–89, 119–22, 181–82; purchasing, 35, 59–61. *See also* tack
equitation: about, 63–64; backing up your horse, 78–79, 92; hands, 68–71; legs, 64–66; seat, 66–68; side-passing, 80, 92. *See also* cues, hand and leg
etiquette on trail, 138–42
evaluating horses, 29, 30, 32–33
eyesight, horse's, 19
eyes, rider's, 71

F
falling off your horse on trail, 155
farrier care, 109–11, 185
feed changes, 183
feet, horse's, 19, 109–11, 112, 120
feet, rider's, 64–66
fenders, 56
first aid kit for horses, 120, 131, 132–33
flanks, 197
floating teeth, 109, 110
fly masks, 113
following on trail, 137–41, 145

Index

food in trailer, 181, 182
food, packing, 121
foreign footing, 92–93, 126
forging, 58
frisky horses, 154, 180–81

G
gait, 25, 197
gaited breeds, 25–27, 29
girths, 39–40
give and release for bolting horses, 168–70
gloves, 61
GPS system, carrying a, 121
grass grabbing behavior, 162, 163
grazing on grass, 122
grizzly bears, 124
grooming: at end of ride, 135; hoof care, 19, 109–11, 112, 120; preventive, 112–14
ground manners, 14, 30
ground poles, 91
group ride leadership, 145
group riding, 142–45, 188–90
gullet, 42

H
hackamores, 47
halter, packing a, 120
halter-bridle combinations, 44, 50
hand cues, 63, 68–70. *See also* cues, hand and leg; reins
hand equitation, 68–71
hay in parks, 182
head bumper in trailer, 181
headstalls, 49–52
head tossing behavior, 162–64
health and safety on trail: about, 122; animal threats, 123–25; checking vital signs, 117–18, 131–33; cooling out, 133–35; etiquette, 138–42; heat exhaustion and dehydration, 126–31; helmets, 60, 61; human threats, 123; lameness, tying up, or colic, 131; natural hazards, 122–23; safety stirrups, 56; trail conditions, 125–26. *See also* veterinarians
health of your horse: age versus, 15–16; evaluating problems, 33; importance of, 17–19
heart monitors, 117–18
heart rate or pulse check, 132
heat exhaustion, 126–31

heatstroke, signs of, 128–29
helmets, 60, 61
herd-bound behaviors: about, 14; barn-sour horses and, 157–58; rider as herd leader, 153–54; riding with experienced pair, 137–38; solo riding versus, 145–49
high line, 198
hikers, 178
hilly terrain, 18, 75–77, 116–17
hobble, 15, 198
hole punch, 50
hoof boots, 110, 120
hoof care, 19, 109–11, 112
hoof picks, 112, 120
horn, 39, 198
horn bags, 54–55
hornets, 123
horse campgrounds, 183–84
horseshoes, 109–11
hosing off your horse, 128, 135
human activities, desensitizing for, 101
human threats on trail, 123
hunting season considerations, 59

I
icy conditions, 110–11, 126
identification, carrying, 119–20
ill-fitting equipment, horse's response to, 112, 152
independence from herd, 14
insect repellents, 113–14
interstate transit requirements, 185

J
jackets or slickers, 61
jeans for riders, 59, 60
jigging, 141, 164–67
jogging, 66

K
Kentucky Mountain Saddle Horses, 25–26
kicking horses, red tail ribbon for, 144–45

L
lameness, 131
laws for horses on roads, 105–6
leading on trail, 137–38, 140, 141–42, 145
lead rope, packing a, 120
leather tack, 52, 53

Index

leather versus synthetic saddles, 38, 39
leg cues, 63, 64–65. *See also* cues, hand and leg
leg equitation, 64–66
leg protection, 186. *See also* boots for horses
leg soundness, 19
leg wraps, 181
lessons for riders: in equitation, 163; in giving cues to your horse, 152–53; in posting, 68; for riding gaited horses, 25; training for endurance events, 117. *See also* riding pointers; trainers
leverage bits, 44, 45, 46–47, 50, 70–71
local trails, 175–78
logs on trail, 78
longeing before trailering, 180–81
longe line, 199
longe line posting lessons, 68
long trot, 116
loping, 66, 199
lung capacity, 19

M

maintenance. *See* preventive maintenance; veterinarians
manure scooper, 182
martingales, 54
mechanical hackamores, 47
medical ID, carrying, 120
mineral blocks, 115–16
Missouri Fox Trotters, 26
Morgans, 22
mountain bikers, 178
mountain lions, 124–25
mounted orienteering events, 190
mounting from the ground, 72–75
mouth care, 109, 163
mouthpieces, 44, 199. *See also* bits
moving object desensitization, 101–6
mud, desensitizing for, 101
Mustangs, 23

N

nagging legs, 65
National Trails Day, 177
natural hazards, 122–23
natural water sources, 129
navicular disease, 19, 199
neck reining, 69–70
neighbor's activities, desensitizing for, 101

night riding, 125–26
noise desensitization, 101
nutritional supplements, 115–16
nylon tack, 52, 53

O

obstacles on trail: navigating over or around, 77–80; poisonous plants or snakes, 122–23; practicing for, 90–93; scary objects, 14, 93–98, 171–73
one-stop rein, 168–70
one-time sponsored group rides, 188–90
orienteering events, 190
out-of-state travel, 185

P

packing for the trail, 88–89, 119–22, 181–82
pain, horse's response to, 151
Paint Horses, 21
parties, desensitizing for, 101
Paso Finos, 26
passing on trail, 143
pavement, riding on, 106
Peruvian Pasos, 26
planned rides, 188–90
plastic bags, desensitizing for, 94–95
pocket knife, carrying a, 120
poisonous plants or snakes, 122–23
poker rides, 190
pommel, 40, 200
pooper-scoopers, 182
ports, 46
posting, 66–68
preparing for trips: about, 109; conditioning program, 115–18; packing, 88–89, 119–22, 181–82. *See also* health and safety
prepurchase exam, 20, 33
preserving trails, 176–78
preventive maintenance: cooling out, 128, 133–35; farrier, 109–11, 185; grooming, 112–14, 135; veterinary care, 109, 152
private land, riding across, 176–77
proof of ownership, 185
pulley rein, 168–70
pulse check, 132
purchasing equipment, 35, 59–61. *See also* tack
purchasing trail horses, 20, 29–33, 154

Q
Quarter Horses, 21–22
Quarter Horse saddletrees, 40

R
rearing behavior, 170
red ribbons in tail, 144–45
reflective tack, 59
reins: antigrazing reins, 162; draw reins, 54; head tossing from improper holding, 163; on hilly terrain, 75; pulley rein, 168–70; tying horse by, 50; types of, 52–53; while riding, 68–71
relaxing in the saddle, 66
repelling insects, 113–14
resources, 191–94
respiration rate, 132
ride and tie events, 190
riders: demeanor with horses, 87–88; etiquette on trail, 138–42; experienced, 63–64, 137–42; falling off on trail, 155; fitness of, 118–19; inexperienced, 14, 46–47, 152–53, 163; size of, 20; tretches for, 80–85. *See also* lessons for riders
riding pointers: for branches over trail, 78; from experienced friends, 137–42; for group rides, 142–45, 188–90; for hills, 18, 75–77, 116–17; for logs on trail, 78; mounting from the ground, 72–75; at night, 125–26; for roads, 104–6; for solo riding, 145–49; for water crossings, 77–78, 98–101, 144, 145. *See also* cues, hand and leg; equitation
ringbone, 19, 200
roads, riding on, 104–6
Rocky Mountain Horses, 26–27
romal reins, 52, 53
rubber grip reins, 53

S
saddlebags, 54–55
saddle bars, 40, 43
saddle fenders, 200
saddle fitters, 42
Saddle Horses, 25–26, 27
saddle pads, 39–40, 42
saddles: about, 35–36; fit and placement, 36, 40–44; in-the-saddle stretches, 80–85; safety stirrups, 56; seat cushions, 37, 55, 56; seat of, 42; signs of poor fit, 112, 152; types of, 37–40
saddle skirts, 200
saddletrees, 40–41
safety. *See* health and safety on trail
Safety Equipment Institute (SEI), 61
safety stirrups, 56
salt blocks, 115–16
scary objects, 14, 93–98, 171–73
seat bones, 66
seat cushions, 37, 55, 56
seat equitation, 66–68
seat of saddle, 42
SEI (Safety Equipment Institute), 61
semiannual vet check, 109, 152
serpentine maneuver, 165–66
shanks, 45, 46–47
shipping boots, 181
shirts for riders, 59, 60
side-passing, 80, 92
snaffle bits, 44–46, 50, 51, 70–71
snakes, 122–23
snow pads, 111
snowy conditions, 111, 126
sociability, 31
solo riding, 145–49
soundness, 17, 19
splint, 201
splint boots, 58–59, 122
split ear headstalls, 49–50
split reins, 52–53
spooking, 170–73
sport boots, 58–59, 122
Spotted Saddle Horses, 27
spurs, 54
staging areas at parks, 178, 179
Standardbreds, 24
state laws, horses on roads and, 105–6
stirrups, 56
stools for mounting, 74
streams, drinking from, 129
stride, 201
strollers, desensitizing for, 95
studs for snow conditions, 111
sunscreen, carrying, 121
surprises, recovery from, 13
sweep riders, 145
synthetic versus leather saddles, 38, 39

T
tack: about, 35–36; breast collars, 56, 57; cruppers, 56, 58; leg protection, 58–59; preventive maintenance, 112; reins, 52–53, 54; sad-

dlebags, 54–55; for safety in hunting season, 59;
training aids, 54. *See also* bridles; saddles
teeth care, 109, 110
temperament: about, 11–14; age versus, 15–16; hereditary aspects of, 20
temperature, horse's, 132–33
Tennessee Walking Horses, 29
terminology, 195–202
Thoroughbreds, 24, 25
throatlatch, 50
thrush, 112
ticks, 114
tie-downs, 54
tired horses, signs of, 129
Tom Thumb bits, 44, 45, 46–47
traditional hackamores, 47
trail bells, 124
trail conditions, 125–26
trailering, 33, 178–82, 185–86
trailers, checking, 181
trail gear, desensitizing for, 88–89
trail horses: attributes of, 11, 13–14, 154; experienced, 15–16, 29–30, 137–42; health of, 15–19, 129;
purchasing, 20, 29–33, 154. *See also* behavior problems; breeds; desensitization
trail maintenance, 176–78
trail obstacles: navigating over or around, 77–80; poisonous plants or snakes, 122–23; practicing for, 90–93; scary objects, 14, 93–98, 171–73
trail riding groups, 142–45, 188–90
trails: local, 175–78; trailering out to, 178–82, 185–86
trail saddles, 36, 37
trail trials, 190
trainers: for bolting habit, 168–70; for bucking horses, 170; finding, 16–17; for horse's random backing, 167; for rearing horses, 170; for remediating bad habits, 153; for trailering, 179
training: about, 14–17; leading and following, 137–38, 140; signs of inadequate, 152; for solo riding, 145–49. *See also* aids; cues, hand and leg
treeless saddles, 40–41
tree-saver ties, 176
trotting, 66–68, 116

trust, horse's level of, 14, 153–54
turn on forehand, 158
turn on haunches, 158
twine, packing, 121
tying up (stiffness), 131
tying your horse: evaluating a horse for, 30; halter-bridle combinations for, 44, 50; safety considerations, 179, 183

U
ulcers, 151

V
vaccinations, 185
vehicle desensitization, 101
veterinarians: for analyzing horse's diet, 155; for choosing a horse, 17; for colic, 131; for conditioning program, 115–16; for emergencies in trail area, 184; for evaluating long-term health issues, 19; pre-purchase exam, 20, 33; semiannual maintenance, 109, 152; for tying up, 131; for vital signs out of range, 133
vital signs, checking, 117–18, 131–33
voice commands, 72

W
warning signs of impending blow up, 155
washing off hot horses, 128, 135
wasps, 123
water bottle, carrying a, 121
water crossings, 77–78, 98–101, 144, 145
water flavorings, 184
waterproof jackets, 61
water sources, 129–31, 181, 184
weather considerations, 126, 155
western headstalls, 49–50
western reins, 52–53
western saddles, 36, 37, 39, 40
withers, 44, 202
workouts, curing barn-sour horses with, 160–61